REASON AND DOCTRINE

REASON AND DOCTRINE

TIME FOR CHRISTIANS TO RETHINK WHAT THEY BELIEVE

TONY DEVANEY MORINELLI

Algora Publishing
New York

Library of Congress Cataloging-in-Publication Data —

Names: Morinelli, Tony Devaney, author.
Title: Reason and doctrine : time for Christians to rethink what they believe / Tony
    Devaney Morinelli.
Description: New York: Algora Publishing, 2016. | Includes bibliographical
    references and index.
Identifiers: LCCN 2016001482 (print) | LCCN 2016001798 (ebook) | ISBN
    9781628942019 (soft cover: alk. paper) | ISBN 9781628942026 (hard cover:
    alk. paper) | ISBN 9781628942033 (pdf)
Subjects: LCSH: Faith and reason—Christianity. | Theology.
Classification: LCC BT50 .M624 2016 (print) | LCC BT50 (ebook) | DDC 230—dc23
LC record available at http://lccn.loc.gov/2016001482

Printed in the United States

Table of Contents

PREFACE

> And every one who hears these words of mine and does not
> do them will be like a foolish man who built his house upon the
> sand; and the rain fell, and the floods came, and the winds blew
> and beat against that house, and it fell; and great was the fall of it."
> (Matthew 7: 26–27)

Contemporary works on biblical and religious scholarship fill vast libraries. They are essential texts for those who take the time invest themselves in a fuller understanding of religious history, practice and belief. Yet, I would propose that there are few other studies that consider Christian doctrines as this book attempts to do. My point of consideration is very simple and very direct: Christian doctrines make no rational sense. When we consider Christian doctrines afresh and apply simple common sense, we must immediately recognize the impossibilities that Christian doctrines pretend as truths. *Reason and Doctrine* attempts to awaken today's Christians to a higher consciousness, to jar the unconscious believer into the realization of Christian doctrines as impossible and irrational concepts that they have unquestioningly accepted through habit or conditioning or simple indifference.

While these questions may seem antagonistic, I assure the reader that I have no animosity towards the social and philosophical aspects of Christianity. The Christian Church is the backbone of Western culture. She is the mother of our learning, of our charitable institutions and even in no small measure the genitrix of our social and political structure. Still, I believe it is time to make the next step in the evolution of Christian thought.

AN APPEAL TO THE READER

PREMISE

In 1637 the great French rationalist René Descartes published his unparalleled "Discourse on the Method of Rightly Conducting the Reason and Seeking Truth in the Sciences." Descartes begins his essay with this observation.

> Common sense[1] is, of all things among men, the best shared; for everyone thinks himself to be so well provided with it, that those even who are the most difficult to satisfy in everything else, do not usually desire more of it than they already have. ... [But] it is not enough to have common sense. The point is to apply it well. The greatest minds are as capable of the greatest vices as they are of the greatest good.

The goal of *Reason and Doctrine* is to challenge today's Christian, a person like any other who believes herself or himself to be possessed of sufficient common sense and intellect to bring Christian doctrine under the scrutiny of that common sense. As Descartes notes, we are normally so satisfied with our common sense that we do not think we require more than we already have. Yet, as the philosopher points out, to have common sense is not sufficient. Common sense must be applied to our understanding of all that we think and believe.

The meaning of the word "common" is essential. In its denotative form the word "common" speaks of something that is familiar to all: something that is shared by all. Thus, "common" sense is precisely that simple knowledge of the physical world in which we live. It is a shared knowledge of the universe, a shared

---

[1] French: "Le bon sens."

sense of the history of humankind, a familiar and general comprehension of nature and how it functions. Common sense provides us with those things we do not normally need to consider before acting. We know without deep reflection that if we drop something it will fall. We know without great debate that fire is hot and ice is cold. In our daily lives we hold a base set of knowledge, a common sense that is so deeply embedded in our intellect that this knowledge does not usually need to be examined continually. For most quotidian applications, it is not necessary to probe our fundamental concepts of the universe to test their validity.

When it comes to religion, however, most Christians do not apply that same common sense to religious doctrines. We fail to test what we believe in faith against the basic truths of what we know of the universe in which we live. In this failure we allow ourselves to commit an affront to human reason and intellect.

For, as Descartes notes, to *possess* common sense is not sufficient, we must *apply* it correctly. If we do not make proper use of that common sense when it comes to matters of religion, we risk embracing the greatest errors: errors that we hold as truths in a blind acceptance of Christian doctrine. What I hope to provoke in this book is the incentive to apply our common sense to what Christians believe about sin, redemption, resurrection and other notions that are rationally untenable and contradict all we know of the world and universe in which we participate. Thus, *Reason and Doctrine* thus boldly sets out the dichotomy between what contemporary Christians profess in faith and what they rationally know of the world.

In many cases Christians have followed Church doctrines that they have held from birth and that they maintain into maturity through the simple fact of having been born to them. There is little or no consideration of their meanings or implications. Even those who have taken some time to give serious thought to the investigation of Christian doctrine often do not open themselves to the full realization of their implications. While such persons may have earnestly attempted investigating the history and development of doctrine, there may often be a reluctance to fully integrate enlightened reason into their observations in order to give sight to blind belief.

Perhaps the unwillingness to move beyond doctrine results from fear of losing the emotional comfort such doctrines provide. Christian doctrine does offer comfort and stability in moments of tranquility as well as moments of trouble. Perhaps there may be psychological reasons where the fear of dismissing the illogic of doctrine subdues any thought of intellectual individuation and freedom. There can also be little doubt that the spiritual formation of many Christians is based on personal notions of guilt and of unworthiness. The sentiments of human guilt and little self-worth have been integral to sermons from the Christian pulpit, from Augustine to Calvin. Do not such orations continue in our time, in the preaching of modern day fundamentalists and evangelicals? How often have we seen the televangelist raise his bible high in his right hand while crying out, "Jesus, I am a sinner!"? The approach to the role of human sinfulness in traditional denominations may be more subtle than that of the fundamentalists, but it is still elemental to the Christian faith. From Amish shunning to Roman Catholic excommunication, the submission of the individual person's to the authority of the Church was indeed the backbone of Christianity in America up to and perhaps including the present day.[1]

Equally disturbing is that among many Christian sects, not only are intellect and reason set aside when considering Christian doctrine, but they are actually misused: particularly concerning scripture. How many churches hold bible study meetings where the proper analysis of scripture in its own right is grossly subverted? How often among such groups do participants invest their time not in a rational historical and literary investigation of biblical texts but instead pore over verses in search of arcane and cryptic codes in the vain hope of discovering some mystical or divine message intended only for those "with eyes to see"[2]? We have to wonder at the human need for the mythical and mystical when we consider such pointless endeavors. Why does this need overrun logic and reason? After all, why would these scriptural sleuths not prefer to discover the truth of the bible's actual history as a significant cultural text rather than to conjure the mythical angels and demons of their imaginations?

DEFINITION OF 'DOCTRINE' IN THIS STUDY

For the purpose of this study, *Reason and Doctrine* will make a distinction between Christian doctrine and Christian teachings. While some readers may find this distinction arbitrary and self-contradictory, the distinction will not only become evident but will be an essential consideration in this book's final chapter. In the strictest sense, the definition of the word

---

[1] Today's adults raised in the Latin Roman service will well remember two prayers that were a constant reminder of one's miserable state. In the *Confiteor* (I Confess), the breast was struck with the clenched fist while repeating with each strike, "Mea culpa. Mea culpa. Mea maxima culpa." Before reception of Communion, the faithful recited with head bowed, "Oh Lord, I am not worthy that Thou shouldst come under my roof." (The hymn with the same text was a well-known standard.)

[2] "Having eyes do you not see, and having ears do you not hear?" Mark 8:18.

"doctrine" is something that is "taught." Etymologically the term derives from the Latin "docere," "to teach." For the purpose of this study, however, the word doctrine does not refer to Christian teachings in the broad social sense. In this study what I term doctrines are those theological beliefs that are held as foundational tenets of faith in the main branches of Christianity. The doctrines to be considered are such tenets as Original Sin, the blood redemption of the cross, the Resurrection and the Ascension.

On the other hand there are, for the purpose of this study, what I will call Christian *teachings*. These are not doctrines but values: values that deal with social and philosophical notions such as love for humankind and concern for the common welfare. While these teachings are not the subject of this study in themselves, I will devote the final chapters to a consideration of their roles in today's world. The distinctions that I make may not be agreeable to all critics and readers. I am sure that for many, doctrines and teachings are inseparable. Yet, these are my definitions and distinctions as used in this text. I do not impose them anywhere else beyond these pages. I must also note that the doctrines that I will cover in this book do not entertain those theological notions that evolved from what I will call the parent doctrines discussed here. Once the irrational aspect of the parent doctrines becomes evident, those doctrines that evolved from them become intrinsically meaningless. Thus, in this text I do not consider such doctrines as the Trinity, or angels or demons. These doctrines all developed from parent doctrines. Once we have discussed the parent doctrines from a rational point of view, consideration of subsequent doctrines renders their individual exploration unnecessary.

I likewise do not treat doctrines such as The Assumption of the Virgin or Mary Theotokos[1] (Mother of God), or any other Marian doctrines, since these doctrines are somewhat specific to the Roman or Orthodox branches of Christianity and have for the most part already been rejected by Protestant Churches.

---

[1] I must make note that one of the most misunderstood Marian doctrines is that of the Immaculate Conception. The Immaculate Conception has nothing whatsoever to do with the conception of Jesus in a virgin mother.
The Immaculate Conception refers to Mary's conception in her mother Anne. If Mary was going to be the mother of Jesus, the mother of God, she clearly could not have been tainted by Original Sin. The divine certainly cannot be housed in the sinful. By some kind of divine grace Mary we therefore determined to have been conceived in her mother Anne without the taint of Original Sin. It is her conception that was immaculate (that is "without the spot" of sin). Continuing this rare exception, since Mary had no Original Sin she would not be subject to death. Thus, Mary did not die. She experiences a "dormition," a "sleep." Upon that sleep Mary was assumed bodily into heaven. This is the doctrine of the Assumption of the Virgin. The feast of the Assumption in the West is the same day as the feast of the Dormition in the East, August 15.

Maria Theotikos, Hagia Sophia, Istanbul.
The letters to the left that look like MP are the Greek abbreviation of Maria. The letters to the right are an abbreviation for Theos Yiuos, God's Son.

abcgallery.com - Internet's biggest art collection

Murillo, Assumption of the Virgin, c. 1680

Let me set out a brief outline of the doctrines that we will consider in this study. First is the foundational belief that humankind was saved by the shedding of the blood of Jesus. The blood sacrifice doctrine upon which all other doctrines are based is actually the most absurd and irrational. One need simply ask what kind of rational god, if such a being exists, would demand a blood sacrifice. The notion of a blood-demanding god affronts all reason and contradicts the very concept of a god of pure reason.

Joined to this doctrine of blood sacrifice is the doctrine that is the cause for that sacrifice, Original Sin. Christians hold that because of the sin of our mythical parents, Adam and Eve, all humankind must be redeemed by a savior. Now, it must be considered that most educated Christian would readily acknowledge that the story of Adam and Eve is nothing more than a symbolic story. Why then do these same Christians who recognize the Adam and Eve tale as myth subscribe to the notion that this couple was guilty of a sin that was passed on to all human creation?

While today's Christian may claim that the sin of Adam and Eve as recounted in scripture is mere story-telling, these same Christians directly profess belief in the misdoings of these mythical ancestors in the subsequent religious doctrines they hold as inviolate. Not only do they subscribe to them in their attestation of doctrines of faith, but they celebrate them in various rituals. Christians demonstrate a practicing belief in the fall of the Adam and Eve mythical archetypes in everything from baptisms to communions to the celebration of Good Friday and Easter. All such ceremonies and events are based on something that never took place: Original Sin.

This doctrine then compounds itself into other irrational beliefs. Because of this Original Sin, committed by non-existent ancestors and therefore not committed, Christian doctrine holds that all humankind requires a redeemer whose blood will wash that sin away. Yet, can there be any notions that are more irrational and improbable than a human blood sacrifice?

The next doctrine that contradicts all we know of life and the universe in which we live is the doctrine of the Resurrection. Turning to the impossible doctrine of the Resurrection, I would ask today's Christian who has any cognizance of the nature of life if there was ever a time when any living thing did not know death. Clearly not. Death is as integral to existence as life. Yet, does today's Christian apply that awareness of life and death each Easter with the celebration of the Resurrection and the promise of the restoration of all humankind to life from death? For some unfathomable reason, all the intellectual power humans possess is left behind at that springtime Easter Sunday ritual. Instead, on that day, Christians rejoice in the delirium of myth and wishful thinking.

The celebration of Easter does have a cultural value. The sentiments expressed in the Easter ritual are among our most primal. Easter is the spring. It is the celebration of rebirth. Easter, like its progenitor, Passover, is a crossing over from winter's gray mourning to spring's vernal vitality. It is a feast to be cherished for its roots in our deepest sentiments. There is not, however, a reason to read its symbolism as the doctrinal truth of a resurrected Jesus.

Coupled with the doctrine of the resurrection is the equally impossible notion of an ascension of the risen dead into heaven. This doctrine overtly offends all common sense and reason. One needs only to ask oneself, "where can a physical body possibly go in the universe as we know it to be?" At the time of the invention of the ascension doctrine over two thousand years ago, such a concept may indeed have seemed plausible. The ancient world believed that above the earth was a realm where the gods lived and to where the risen body would ascend. In Paul's mind, the risen Jesus ascended into a heaven where he sat enthroned in a very real physical space above the clouds. From that celestial throne he would one day descend to gather up the faithful. Fundamentalist Christians and televangelists make great drama of that moment which they call "The Rapture," a topic to be discussed in Chapter 7. While we can easily excuse and even justify this notion when it comes to Paul and the world in which he lived, such a belief today is manifestly untenable. Cannot the average Christian apply what is known of the physical universe to the irrational and unscientific ideas of the doctrines of the resurrection and ascension to immediately recognize that they are more than deeply flawed? Since the time of Galileo, we have known that above the earth there are no celestial realms but only the infinite universe. There is simply no place for a physical body to go.

Reason and Doctrine also points out those Christian doctrines that not only contradict all that is rational but that also have no foundation in scripture. This study clearly delineates the distinct errors made by Paul in his readings of Genesis and in his interpretation of Jesus as a blood sacrifice. We also consider the various faces of Jesus as portrayed in the gospels and the epistles. Most Christians see Jesus as single personality with a given and fixed set of teachings. Nothing could be further from the truth. Even a casual reading of the New Testament will quickly reveal that there are at least four different faces to Jesus, often faces with little resembles to each other.

This book then ventures into a degree of reasoned speculation to make its most daring claim. Having dismissed all notions of Jesus as a blood sacrifice for human salvation, Reason and Doctrine asks what then would have been the reason for his death on the cross. What did Jesus actually preach that was so dangerous? Who did Jesus think he was? Chapter 9 proposes that Jesus truly did think himself to be a king and that he was justifiably crucified for political reasons. While the notion may at first appear to be somewhat sensationalist, I can assure the reader that it is not so intended. The proposal is grounded with unbiased scriptural reference and it is no different than other current conjectural thoughts that Jesus was an apocryphal prophet or that he was a simple itinerant preacher or that he was a social revolutionary.

To conclude my appeal to the reader, and in the spirit of full disclosure, I must note that I am not a specialist in biblical scripture—although I have taught the bible as literature for over thirty years. My background is primarily in medieval hagiography (saints' lives), another text-based discipline that deals with deciphering and interpreting multiple manuscript versions of comparable historical or fictional accounts. I am accustomed to working with ancient texts and to deciphering them both literally and interpretively.[1] I have spent no small number of hours with gloved hands

---

[1] For those interested, you may find two of my translations online at Fordham University Medieval Sourcebook, *The Life of Saint Julian Hospitaller* and *The Seven Sleepers of Ephesus*.

armed with a wooden spatula going over page after page of parchment or vellum.[1] The kaleidoscope of paleography is no stranger to me.

I would also note that I am not a scholar in biblical languages. My knowledge of Hebrew and Septuagint Greek is what I would call linguistic. With my background in the Romance languages in their current and ancient forms, I have a structural knowledge of the languages of the bible and can certainly read their alphabets. When I make use of Hebrew or Greek, it is for the sake of denotative clarity. When I find that I have a question about the meaning of a word, I make use of Strong's Concordance.[2] For references to the patristic writers, I have used online sites that provide direct access to early Christian documents.[3] For quotations from scripture I use the online *Blue Letter Bible*, which offers immediate access and ease of transcription to numerous translations.

I also announce that *Reason and Doctrine* has no interest in those current debates on such topics as to whether Jesus was an apocalyptic preacher or a social reformer. *Reason and Doctrine* does not concern itself with whether or not Jesus was an historical and real person. This question has no effect on the points proposed in this book. While I personally hold that there was indeed a man called Jesus, the historical and provable evidence of his existence is not the question of this text. Whether there was or was not an historical Jesus does not alter the questions of this study. Today's Christians believe that Jesus existed. It is their belief that counts. Indeed, it is that belief in Jesus that is the groundwork of all the doctrines and teachings of Christianity. My concern is the influence of this man, real or imagined, on the entire development of the Western world. The scope and power of that influence is beyond the ability of any single text. Nonetheless, there are certain specific doctrinal implications that merit some consideration.

The core of these doctrines is set out in the very creeds of most Christian Churches: the Nicene Creed, the Apostle's Creed and the Athanasian Creed. The doctrines of these creeds as pronounced by Christians around the world are nothing short of professions of irrational commitments to notions of impossible myths. The creeds profess belief in such phenomena as virgin births and ascents into a heavenly realm.

---

[1] When a researcher requests access to an ancient text in addition to documents, the library may also set very stringent rules. The requester is to present letters attesting to the scholarity of the researcher. Once the background of the researcher is acknowledged and access to the manuscripts is permitted, the library will require that the investigator wear gloves when examining the requested texts and that the pages of the text be turned not by hand but by a wooden spatula.

[2] Dr. James Strong, a professor of exegetical theology at Drew Theological, published his "Exhaustive Concordance of the Bible" in 1890. For the purpose of this book, I find his work on the etymology of biblical terms most helpful.

[3] See my bibliography.

This text hopes to appeal to simple reason and does not require a deep knowledge of complex theology, ancient history or even of scripture. This is not to say that these areas of study are not important or that they do not serve the writing of this text. Indeed, *Reason and Doctrine* is fully documented and grounded in scholarly investigation. To reiterate, scholarship alone is not the only foundation of this book, it is rather, as Descartes advises, the application of common sense and reason. Thus, the intent of *Reason and Doctrine* is to provoke questions of the average Christian that are for the most part rarely considered.

BACKGROUND

The premise of *Reason and Doctrine* came to me during a Holy Week service: Good Friday to be precise. It came to me in what I would call an intellectual burst of light: a moment of personal illumination not unlike Paul's conversion on the road to Damascus. Here I was in Philadelphia, in the beautiful white box pews of one of the country's oldest Anglican Episcopal churches. The church was warm with the faint smell of candle wax, but in keeping with First Friday as a day of mourning, there were no flowers. After the reading of the Passion, the congregation solemnly approached the altar to reverence the cross held out in the hands of the priest as the a capella choir (there is no organ on Good Friday) intoned Bach's hauntingly beautiful, *"Oh sacred head sore wounded, defiled and put to scorn. O kingly head surrounded by crown of piercing thorn."*

Suddenly, enraptured by the music as I was, and inwardly moved by the communal ceremony, an uncalled for thought ruptured my minor ecstasy. By some odd intermingling of sight and sound, the sight of a woman on her knees before the cross kissing the feet of the crucified Jesus stunned me. The sight of the woman became something of a transcendental revelation. While the intoxicating minor harmonies of the choir embraced her and the procession of petitioners waited solemnly behind her, my reason pierced through the moment to see the horror of this ritual. The obscene violence of the devotion and of the musical text struck like a thunderbolt. What were we doing? Why were we all so taken by this image of torture and blood and human sacrifice? Certainly, this was not something to sing about. This death ritual was not something to embrace. Something was clearly wrong here.

Then, out of my confusion and consternation there was a moment of revelation. Immediately, the question came to me, "What kind of god, particularly one that is characterized as a god of pure reason, would demand a blood sacrifice?" "Why was I in this church singing along and celebrating acts of vengeance, cruelty and violence?" "Why were reasonable and rational and highly educated adults falling to their knees to kiss an image of blood-stained feet fixed to a cross?" The choir continued; the music all the more hypnotic: "*In thy most bitter passion, my heart to share doth cry, with thee for my salvation upon the cross to die.*" Verse after verse the hymn seduced with its alluring yet innately sadistic appeal to physical suffering, blood and death. The poetry of the verse, raised to greater heights by the captivating music of Bach, subverted all reason. Struggling against the hymn's seduction, my reason spoke out. My reason, reining in my emotional response to the music, pointed out the implausible, illogical and repellent situation that the hymn described.

Then, as only the reason of a child can perceive, my younger daughter, seeing this line of adults kissing the cross, asked me, "Dad, do I have to do that?" The lightning inside my head flashed again. The spiraling melodic line of the hymn battled against the simple steps of reason. In an undifferentiated exchange, the arguments of reason and sentiment cross fired inside me. Like a fireworks display in what I believe is called a "fountain," one bursting spark sets off another in a succession of sizzling cascades. Question after question simultaneously exploded in my head. They were explosions of illumination. Bombs bursting in air that shattered everything I thought about god and religion: ideas that I had held without doubt. The experience was eruptive and invigorating, an intellectual rush. I, like Paul being dashed from his horse, was experiencing a personal illumination. Suddenly, I knew that nothing in this hymn, nothing in this ceremony made any sense: sacred head, crown of thorns, scorn, wounds, bleeding! Why was I in a state of joyful sorrow, singing about death and blood and human suffering? My intonations and that of the church were celebrating a murderous god who demanded the sacrifice of human blood. This was sadomasochism developed into art. Where was my head? What was I doing? How could this be? Where was my common sense?

Desperately seeking some logic to this conundrum, I moved to what I had been told and had believed was the cause of such death and suffering: the need to save me and everyone else from sin. Save me from what sin? Yes, I did wrong things. Yet, how were any of my singular and personal transgressions (or for that matter how were the wrong doings of humankind as a whole) the cause of crucifying a Jewish prophet two thousand years ago? Are all the petty crimes, the wars, and the killings, the cruelties and insanities of the human race, summed up and compensated in the condemnation and execution of a single man in ancient Roman Palestine? Is the measured sum of all human foibles weighed and repaid in the barbaric punishment of one man? Is there a ratio of shed blood and suffering flesh measured out to compensate and appease a vengeful god for centuries of human transgressions? Any such notion defies all reason.

It is time for today's Christian to apply common sense and to apply it well. It is time to ask the question, "How does the death of one man for the misdeeds of all human history reflect any sense of balance or justice?" Furthermore, if there is such an entity as a god, why would this being demand the blood death of one man as a justification for all humanity? More than that, why would this god particularly demand the blood of an innocent victim? If compensation were necessary would not a god, who is supposed to be the ultimate rational being, find a less savage method to set things right? Furthermore, what is the rationale of a god who addresses himself with such attention to this singular blood lust? Would not a rational god address himself instead to some purposeful and positive method to ameliorate the general condition of the humankind he supposedly created?

These simple common sense questions and their rational answers hit me strongly. Why would a god demand a blood sacrifice? A rational god, a god of reason and intellect who needs the blood of his very own creation, even to satisfy some kind of divine justice, makes no sense. In a domino effect, the collapse of the logic of one doctrine set into motion a chain reaction that set off a series of other questions. If a god who demands blood makes no sense, why do I need the victim whose blood is shed? If the need for a victim makes no sense, why do I need a personal savior? Then, in addition, I realized that the notion of being saved was dubious. What is he saving me from? Furthermore, who is this savior? Who was this man who taught in the towns of Roman Palestine? How can a god come to earth? Why would a god come to earth? Furthermore, what of this man-god's other attributes? What is the meaning and purpose of virgin births, of resurrections from the dead, of ascents into heaven! What were these ideas all about? How can they make any sense?

I also had to ask myself: Would it not seem that a creator god might seek to contribute to the life and to the vitality of what he created? The notion of a god who seeks death is intrinsically contradictory to the notion of a god who gives life. Was this a two-faced god: a god who created only to destroy, a god who seemed to relish the latter more than the former?

As the inky shadows of the illogic of the doctrines floated aimlessly and shapelessly in my head, I heard other voices. The writings of such as Darwin and Einstein and Sagan and Hawking, and many others, began whispering to me. How do the religious doctrines of Christianity confront what we know of an infinite universe and the evolution of humankind? Oh yes, well-educated and sophisticated Christians ostensibly have no problem merging religion with science. Yet, in practice and in fact do they really? The answer is "no."

The accommodation of religion with science is only partial and superficial. It does not get to the root of doctrinal irrationalism.

As I sat listening to the Good Friday service I became more perplexed. As I watched the stripping of the altar, the ripping away of all things physical, questions churned in my head. All my knowledge of the world in which we live collided with what I had thoughtlessly accepted in church. As the altar was laid bare, so too my mind was stripped of religious doctrine's mythical coverings.

The realization of my blindness towards the irrationality of Christian doctrines was actually something of an intellectual embarrassment. After all, I considered myself a rather well-educated individual. I hold a doctorate from one of the most prestigious colleges in America; I speak several modern languages and read several ancient and classical. My knowledge of literature and history is quite thorough, and while I may not be able to quote chapter and verse, I am well read in the Bible. Indeed, the Bible has captivated me since childhood. As an adult I have been an avid reader of popular biblical commentaries from the books of Raymond Brown and Dominic Crossan to Bart Ehrman and Richard Carrier. Yet, I had never thought to integrate all the disciplines of my intellectual background with what went on in church. There was, in effect, an intellectual separation of church and the natural state, a conflict between the sacred and the profane, between emotion and reason. It was time to take full stock of my doctrinal predicament.

Rushing to the library, I searched out every text on atheism. I covered them all, from Bertrand Russell to Christopher Hitchens and Richard Dawkins. What I found was that, while these convinced atheists presented clear and compelling arguments, they made their arguments as an assault from outside the Church. In so doing, they neglected any examination from an internal Christian point of view. While I could well appreciate their observations, those observations did not respond to my questions as a practicing Christian. Furthermore, Hitchens and Dawkins, with all due respect, tended towards a rather abrasive if not even insulting approach. Their arguments, strong as they may be, seemed more like attacks than persuasions. Consequently, rather than attract a possible audience, their work might tend to repulse their potential readers before any convincing argument might be made. Dawkins, for one, states from the start that he will not employ biblical reference to state his cause. Yet, to me, biblical reference would be a most logical tool if one wanted to engage and convince the Christian reader. How better to bolster the argument against irrational Christian doctrine than to use the highly relevant material found in the bible and in church tradition to underscore their fallacies? To me, then, biblical reference set against reason and knowledge would be the most logical starting place to engage the Christian reader. If what Dawkins calls "a raising of consciousness" is to take place, the reasoning of the argument must begin from the common point held by all Christians: the New Testament. Arguments without a scriptural base may fail to convince. Moreover, arguments such as those by very vocal atheists that dismiss out of hand any Christian doctrines without biblical reference may only turn aside the desired audience.

How was I to proceed in this study? I did not want to be dismissive of the faith that raised me. If I were going to set aside the doctrines of the Church, I wanted to do it on the Church's grounds. For my own satisfaction I needed to work out the reasons for my rejections of Church doctrines from the very texts that I was rejecting. The process therefore would largely involve a close study of biblical texts and of authors who have devoted a lifetime to biblical scholarship.

In the field of biblical exegesis, there is probably no better mentor for the non-specialist than Bart D. Ehrman. Ehrman opened my eyes to the flaws in the New Testament from a textual perspective. While *Reason and Doctrine* uses scripture to substantiate many of its points, it does so in order to initiate the discussion from a common ground with the traditional Christian. More important, however, than examining Christian doctrine from a scriptural perspective, this text considers many questions from a secular scientific point of view. I would even say that the ultimate rationale for the impossibilities of Christian doctrines derives directly from what we know scientifically of the universe we inhabit: the simplest consideration of which immediately contradicts no small number of Christian doctrines.

Let me review a few examples in history that raised our collective consciousness through human reason. As early as the first half of the sixteenth century, Nicholas Copernicus opened our eyes to the true arrangement of the solar system. In the next generation, Galileo Galilei confirmed it. Yet, the revelation of this arrangement where the earth was no longer the center of all things was not happily received. Galileo faced the Inquisition and was convicted to house arrest and reduced to silence on the subject of his discoveries.[1]

Yet, the notion of a universe in which the earth was not the center, as the bible suggested, was not the only point that troubled the Church. In this new view, the old system of the skies in which the outermost ring was the great Empyrean, the heavenly realm of gods and angels, lost its place. It simply did not exist. Here was the real problem for the Church. If that outermost circle did not exist, if there was no ethereal realm directly above the earth, where then was that place from which angels descended? Similarly, where

---

[1] It was not until 1992 that Pope John Paul II acknowledged the church's regret for prosecuting Galileo.

was that ethereal place to which resurrected bodies and prophets and saints ascended? Clearly, the ancient notion of celestial realms that ringed the earth was impossibility. We have been aware of the nature of the universe since the time of Galileo. Galileo's greater threat to the Church's doctrines was that the universe his telescope revealed left no room for a celestial realm of gods and angels. In a letter to Johannes Kepler, Galileo wrote,

> My dear Kepler, what would you say of the learned here, who, replete with the pertinacity of the asp, have steadfastly refused to cast a glance through the telescope? What shall we make of this? Shall we laugh, or shall we cry? .... Verily, just as serpents close their ears, so do these men close their eyes to the light of truth.[1]

It seems that today's Christians, when looking at the doctrines of their religion refuse, however, to look through the lens of reason. Thus, even today, Christians go along believing in the pre-Copernican idea of an ultimate circle beyond the stars: a heavenly realm above the earth, an Empyrean. Thus, they blindly go on proclaiming the physical ascension of Jesus or the assumption of Mary into that very place which they know intellectually does not and cannot exist. They do not trouble themselves by imposing what they know rationally upon what they choose to believe religiously. In our own era, with the advances of technology, we now see that the universe is a realm of endless expansion filled with countless galaxies. Yet, even with this information, we still do not conclude that notions of a divine space where physical bodies ascend are manifestly impossible.

Then we have the problem of Natural History. On November 22, 1859, a new book appeared for sale: a text entitled *On the Origin of the Species* by Charles Darwin. It was an instant success. The book changed forever our notion of the nature of humankind. In the twenty-first century, most Christians of a certain intellectual background readily acknowledge the principles of evolution. Most mainstream churches, too, acknowledge the validity of Darwin's theory. The educated, intellectual and open-minded Christian accepts Darwin and has no problem with the notion of man's evolution from other species.

Yet, do we really apply what we know intellectually of Darwin's ideas to what we believe theologically of man's supposed fall from grace? Fundamentalists aside, most Christians consider the Genesis story as metaphor. But even as metaphor, the foundation of Christian dogma is centered on a notion of a fall from grace, a fall that demanded redemption. Where, and when in the process of evolution, did this fall take place? Who

---

[1] Letters to Johannes Kepler (1610).

was its cause? Clearly, there never was such an event. Consequently, if there was no fall, there is no need for redemption.

Certainly an atheist would dismiss all such notions of fall and redemption outright as simple-minded myths with no need for further investigation. Fundamentalists and "born-agains" are by definition immune from honest biblical investigation. Nevertheless, neither the confirmed atheist nor the firmly grounded fundamentalist is my intended or expected audiences. My intended reader is the well-educated, rational and informed Christian with an open mind who is willing to consider points that may have hovered lightly in the back of the mind or that through innocent compliance never considered at all. The problem, I think, for the well-educated practicing Christian is that religion is so deeply tied into personal habit and tradition that there is little interest in examining its fundamental teachings at the root. I pose the questions of this book to them.

May I reiterate that while every care has been taken to approach all topics in a careful and scholarly method, *Reason and Doctrine* does not claim to be an academic text. It does not demand knowledge of Hebrew or Greek. It does not even look to a reader who can quote the bible by chapter and verse, although some knowledge of scripture would be helpful. *Reason and Doctrine* requires only a reader with simple reason and common sense who is willing to apply that reason and common sense to the doctrines held as truths by most practicing Christians. In so doing today's Christian cannot help but perceive the glaring and innate fallacies of these doctrines. The questioning Christian will immediately perceive that to apply what is known not only of scriptural history but what is known of the universe in which we live will immediately reveal manifest and indisputable contradictions to church doctrine. After all, Christian doctrines have their origins in a world long past. In that world centuries ago those doctrines may have appeared rational and meaningful. This is certainly no longer the case. What I propose in this book is that the doctrines of Christianity are grounded upon the primitive notions of an ancient world innocently ignorant of its own fabric, a world that organized itself according to the limits of its technical skills and often in mystical and symbolic arrangements, a world that sought to appease angry gods with blood sacrifices and who sought the comfort of mythic fields of eternal happiness: notions that are impossible in a post-Galileo, post-Darwin world.

Readers who are of an evangelical persuasion may not have read this far, if they picked up this book at all. For those others, however, who are willing to engage in a debate between their reason and those Christian dogmas that they may have held, I ask you to stay with this text and follow its step-by-step inquiry. If you are of such a mind as to be able to consider new and unorthodox concepts, you may find that this book suggests no small number of topics worthy of at least some exploration.

What follows is an outline of my chapters. In them, I hope the reader will find a modest attempt at exploring logically and sequentially questions about Christianity and its foundations. As we will see, the doctrines of Christianity not only have little foundation in the scriptures that created them but they affront all reason and understanding: Christian doctrine is Reason and Doctrine (Matthew 7:26).

CHAPTERS OUTLINE

Chapter 1:   Defining the Questions

Chapter 1 sets out the five principal points upon which this study of Christian doctrine is based. These points include: the doctrine of salvation by the blood sacrifice of Jesus, the doctrine that death was introduced to the world by the sin of humankind, the doctrines of the resurrection and the ascension, the question of who Jesus was and what he taught, and finally, the question of the future of Christianity. Chapter 1 questions the origins of these doctrines, as they are poorly established in scripture; but more important, they defy all rational thought and knowledge of the universe in which we live. This chapter suggests that while most educated Christians are quite knowledgeable when it comes to their awareness of the world, they do not apply this knowledge to the rational and scientific impossibilities of Christian doctrines and dogmas.

Chapter 2:   Establishing a Groundwork: Scripture

While a close study of scripture is not the specific goal of this text, reference to scripture is essential to establish certain groundwork when discussing Christian doctrine. To this end I set out, from the start, that I do not hold scripture as inerrant or divinely inspired. Furthermore, much of my understanding concerning scripture as text is based on my own work in medieval literature and in great measure on scholars such as Bart D. Ehrman who have specialized in the field. Chapter 2 then goes on to propose my views on scriptural interpretation, the foundation for that interpretation and various references to substantiate that foundation. We see that many stories found in the New Testament are distinct and unique inventions in their own right and are often peculiar to the gospel or epistle in which they are found. Even so, Christian doctrine has often collated various distinct and disparate tales in order to create a single notion or perception that does not exist in any one story alone.

Chapter 3: "A Servant Set Apart": Paul

Chapter 3 examines the writings of Paul, the first set of texts to lay out what would become the foundations of Christian beliefs: beliefs that ultimately became doctrine. This chapter examines the various contradictions in Paul's own writing and the inconsistencies between Paul's epistles and other books of the New Testament. We look at Paul's conversion to Christianity to find that there is not one story but three—two of which were written by Paul himself, and the third which is found in the book of Acts. An examination of Paul's writings finds no small amount of equivocation. In one passage in particular, Paul openly admits that he has been deceitful for the sake of his mission. Here I suggest that if Paul acknowledges that he has been less than honest in order to achieve his own goals in at least one instance, we may need to ponder whether he can be trusted in his other pronouncements: pronouncements that became the foundation of Christian doctrine and dogma.

Chapter 4: "In the Beginning": Genesis

Most Christians, other than fundamentalists, recognize the story of Genesis as a metaphor, a myth: a literary invention as an attempt to explain the creation. Yet, what most Christians do not realize is that the creation myth of Genesis is not one tale but two. The two tales derive from distinctly different sources and were probably stitched together sometime around the sixth century before the Christian era, when the Old Testament as we now know it was being compiled and edited. The first creation story begins at Genesis 1:1 and continues to Genesis 2:3. The second story runs from 2:4 to 3:24.

I would likewise propose that most Christians do not realize that the distinction between the two stories is easily recognizable by several means. The first indication that we are reading a different tale is that the second story opens with the verse "These are the generations of the heavens and of the earth when they were created, in the day that the Lord God made the earth and the heavens." This verse is clearly an introduction to a new account and not, as some would have it, an elaboration of the first account. The second and more important indication is that each story uses a different word for "God." The creator deity of the first tale is called "God." In the second version he is called "Lord God." Finally, and even more telling, the content of each story is distinctly different. The first is a story in which the creating god sees that all he has done is good and so bestows his blessing on man and beast. The second story, however, is the one in which Adam and

Eve transgress their creator's command and are cast out from their paradise. Therefore, we ask, since there are clearly two stories, one of blessing and one of a curse, why is it that Paul and all those after him have decided to concentrate only on the latter?

Paul's interpretation of Genesis is completely unfounded. He has misread the text. Furthermore, this myth of a lost Paradise and the introduction of death into the world by the singular sin of two imaginary people goes largely unexamined even today. Thus, in its unexamined state, so remains the unquestioned foundation of an entire doctrinal system that has no grounding in reason or common sense.

Chapter 5:   "By Man Came Death": Paul, Adam's Fall and Redemption

Chapter 5 returns to Paul. This chapter shows that Paul has clearly misread Genesis. He has not taken note of the distinction between the two stories. From his misreading Paul invents the notion of the Fall as understood in Christian doctrine. Joined to the notion of the Fall is the misconception that there was a time when humanity did not know death. Clearly, this is an absurdity. There was no time in history when humankind or any other living entity did not know death. Yet, the contemporary, educated Christian well versed in Darwin and other scientific concepts accepts without question, if not intellectually then in practice, the doctrine of a primal world that did not know death. The discussion in Chapter 5 further suggests the need to recognize the reality of death as part of the life process and not as some punishment for the sins of a remote mythic ancestor.

Chapter 6.   "By His Blood": Jesus as Redeemer

Chapter 6 continues the argument of the preceding chapter to consider the notion of Jesus as a blood sacrifice winning redemption for mankind. As the chapter will illustrate there is little in the synoptic gospels that proposes Jesus as a sacrificial redemption. The chapter concludes with the refutation of the most irrational and repulsive of all Christian doctrines, the notion of a blood sacrifice to a vengeful god as the means to redeem the sins of humankind.

Chapter 7:   "The Trumpet Shall Sound": Resurrection and Ascension

Chapter 7 first considers the scriptural accounts of the resurrection of Jesus—only to find that there is little consistency among the various versions. It would seem that, given the implication of such a marvelous event, the details would have been quite impressive and memorable. However, this is apparently not the case. The gospel accounts of the resurrection of Jesus simply do not align. Chapter 7 then considers the notions of resurrection and ascension from a rational point of view. In the ancient world, the heavens were considered a distinct and physical realm that loomed above the circle of the earth. To the mind of antiquity, the gods resided in the sphere just above the firmament that divided their kingdom from that of humankind. Thus, in the universe of the first century, Jesus could not only rise from the dead but he could then ascend into a specific and delimited heaven, a distinct physical place somewhere beyond the clouds. In the first century and for a good many years after, the doctrine of the Ascension would be within the possibilities of belief. In the first half of the 17th century, however, a text was written that documented a certain truth, much to the consternation of the church. This text not only removed the earth from the center of creation but shattered the crystal vaults that walled off the realm of the gods from that of humanity. Still, today, contemporary Christians who fully accept Galileo's universe from an intellectual point completely ignore its implications when it comes to their religion. Furthermore, from the time of Einstein onward, the universe as we know it simply contains no realm for the residence of an ascended physical body. In the plainest terms, Jesus simply had no place to go.

Chapter 8:   "Blessed Are They:" What Did Jesus Actually Teach?

Chapter 8 returns to a consideration of the scriptures, noting that the Jesus of each gospel, written at a different time by a different author, is quite distinct. Each Jesus has an individual and recognizable message. While most Christians believe that the message of the Jesus of the gospels was love, this belief is mistaken. In Mark's gospel, for example, Jesus uses the word love only four times, and these four times are within one single statement, the famous variation on the verse from Deuteronomy. In the same way, Mark's Jesus never utters the Lord's Prayer or delivers the Sermon on the Mount. Only as the gospels evolve does the message of love and concern for others evolve. Was the emphasis on teaching the value of love devised by Jesus or, like so many other things, was it part of Paul's vision? If love was not the primary message of Jesus, what was? In Chapter 8 we will explore this question.

Chapter 9:   "Hail King of the Jews": The Reason for the Crucifixion

Having explored the traditional notions of Jesus' teachings and his subsequent death as an imagined sacrifice to a wrathful god, we now move on to various personal conjectures about Jesus and who he may have thought he was. We first look at the name Jesus meaning "savior." Was this his real name or was it a name given to him by his followers? How did Jesus see himself as the "Christ," the "Messiah" the anointed king? Chapter 8 points out several passages where Jesus and his followers saw him as the promised political king of Israel. As we have noted, to any rational mind Jesus could not have been a blood sacrifice to some vengeful god. If it was not done as a blood sacrifice, then what was the reason for his crucifixion? If Jesus was indeed a political upstart who sought to set himself upon the throne of Israel, was his execution perfectly justified from the Roman perspective?

Chapter 10:   The Teachings of Christianity: "Go and Do Likewise"

As the reader has seen, the preface of this book carefully notes that I have distinguished between Christian doctrine and Christian teaching. Having set aside the irrational doctrines of Christianity in the preceding chapters, Chapter 9 turns to consider the value of Christian teachings in their own right. The chapter looks at several opinions on Christian values, some in favor and some against. A comparison is drawn between this text and the work of Thomas Jefferson, who also sought to distinguish Christian values from Christian doctrines. The chapter concludes with the hope that, while discarding the irrational notions of doctrine, we might maintain the teachings of human values.

Chapter 11:   Conclusion: Christianity and the Future

The final chapter of this book draws together the various notions that I have proposed. I make a final request of the reader to honestly and rationally assess those doctrines that Christianity has taught over the centuries. I also ask for an unbiased assessment of Christian teachings; teachings of concern for humankind that have been the foundation of Western culture. Chapter 10 then concludes the study with the question, "Can we build a house on the stone of reason and intellect and let the waters of superstition and the waves of myth be washed away with the house built on sand?"

Chapter 1. Establishing the Fundamental Questions

An examination of the problems of Christian doctrines first requires establishing which of the many doctrines would best serve as the foundation and starting point. Christian doctrines have developed and evolved in such a way that they are often so closely intertwined that it is difficult to isolate one from another. The doctrine of the resurrection of Jesus, for example, derives from and is integrally connected to doctrine of the salvific value of his death on the cross. Likewise, the doctrine of the ascension develops from the doctrine of the resurrection. In many ways Christian doctrines recall a set of Russian nesting dolls, a *matryoshka*. When you take one of these dolls in hand, the outer appearance is one of a single wooden doll, but then you immediately find that the outer doll opens to reveal another doll inside it. Open that doll and you find yet another, and on it goes to find any number of hidden dolls nestled one inside the other. So too, one Christian doctrine is enclosed within another. This study will attempt to disengage one doctrine from another while at the same time referencing the elements that link them. There will be times, however, when sidetracking will be necessary.

In this chapter I outline essential questions that will be elaborated in subsequent chapters. We'll examine the series of questions on Christian doctrine from two principal points: a secular rational approach and an approach that makes use of Christian scripture. Thus, while this study has as its basis the application of reason and common sense to illustrate the impossibilities of Christian doctrine and dogma, it will also make use of scriptural reference to substantiate its observations. In the final chapter, I hope to establish a distinction between Christian teaching and Christian doctrine. Christian teaching, as I see it, is that collective ethic of social concern and responsibility that developed in the course of human social evolution and that was codified most specifically in the Old and New Testaments. While the fundamental concepts of human ethics may be found in broad perspectives in other religious tenets, they are distinctively associated in the framework of Christianity as developed and expressed particularly in the writings of Paul.

The First Question: "By His Blood"

The first and most fundamental Christian doctrine is that humankind was redeemed from sin and death through the blood sacrifice of Jesus. This principal doctrine is at the heart of all other Christian doctrines and is, by its very nature, the most repugnant.

Can there be anything more barbaric, abhorrent or irrational than blood sacrifice? Is there anything more primitive and more irrational in humankind's collective psyche than the superstitious belief that the gods must be appeased by the slaughter and death of a sacrificial human being or animal? Yet, the belief in this blood sacrifice, and belief in its value, are the foundation of all Christianity: the belief of over two billion otherwise rational people.

How can this be? Not only does today's Christian blindly accept the notion of one man's bloody death as the means of reconciliation with a vengeful god, but the Christian believer goes so far as to embrace this notion lovingly! How is it that Christians raise as the symbol of their faith the image of a torturous and bloody means of execution, the cross? Christians mount this symbol of death atop their churches and along roadsides. They wear the cross as an amulet around the neck. This image of violence may be of silver or gold. It may be ornamented with precious stones. Some Christians sign their bodies with its outline from left to right in the West or right to left in the East. Almost without exception, and despite whatever differences might divide them, all Christian sects would immediately attest that the cornerstone of belief is the image of the cross and what it represents.[1][2] On this cross, over two thousand years ago, Jesus of Nazareth was executed by one of the vilest and most excruciating methods ever devised. What kind of rational god, if such an entity exists, would subject his creation to such a

[1] For some three hundred years following the Reformation, most Protestant sects removed the cross along with nearly all other iconography as representative of what they considered Romanism or popery. Protestant cemeteries rarely used a cross as a grave marker. Although Protestants often sang about the cross, they rarely displayed it. Since the mid 1800s however, the cross has made a come-back. It is not uncommon to find three crosses or a cross draped in purple fabric along our highways. Even so, while Protestants may have reclaimed the cross, you rarely see Protestants display a crucifix: the body of Jesus on the cross.
[2] Two notable exceptions are Jehovah's Witnesses and Church of Latter Day Saints (Mormons), who do not use the image of the cross.

death? Yet, Christian doctrine teaches that on this cross the flesh and blood of Jesus became a full and perfect sacrifice to redeem the sins of humankind.

The epistle of 1 Peter, paraphrasing Isaiah 30:26, proposes that "He himself bore our sins in his body on the tree, that we might die to sin and live to righteousness. By his wounds you have been healed" (2:24). This doctrine of Jesus' blood sacrifice is what all Christians, by definition of being Christian, hold as one of the cornerstones of faith. How few Christians, however, have stepped back from belief to check that belief against reason? How many have truly examined the meaning of the cross, the meaning of the death of Jesus and the very notion of mankind's need to be saved by means of a blood sacrifice? How can any clearly thinking person hold such a blood-thirsty event as the center of religious belief? Such a notion is not merely illogical. Such a notion is repugnant to the rational mind.[1]

Not only is the notion of blood sacrifice irrational and barbaric but even more so is the notion of a god who would demand it. Why would a god, a god who in theory is the embodiment of intellect and reason, require a blood sacrifice? It simply makes no sense. Such a wrathful god contradicts all intelligent and rational value for life and for creation. To believe in such a god is to believe in one of the most primitive of superstitions: that humankind must win the favor of the god, appease him and quell his anger at a very high cost.

How is it that such a primitive notion survives to this day? Nothing expresses this barbarous belief better than the words of the old Protestant hymn, "Nothing but the Blood."

> What can wash away my sin?
> Nothing but the blood of Jesus;
> What can make me whole again?
> Nothing but the blood of Jesus.
> (chorus)
> Oh! Precious is the flow
> That makes me white as snow;
> No other fount I know,
> Nothing but the blood of Jesus.
> (Robert Lowry, 1876)

The text is nothing less than appalling. What could be more primitive or barbarous than the idea of being washed white by the red of blood? Yet, Christians accept this doctrine without the slightest doubt. Even those more

---

[1] It is with some reluctance that I refer to *The Holy Land Experience* of Orlando, Florida. At this travesty, Christians watch in tears and sighs as actors recreate the bloody death of Jesus with the utmost theatrical gore. Such a demonstration is nothing short of an appeal to the fascination with the sadomasochistic.

contemporary believers who may scoff at the fundamentalist Protestant language of this old hymn belie their disregard for what the text says by their very practice of Christian rituals.

Early humankind practiced human sacrifice to appease their gods. At a certain point, however, human sacrifice was replaced by animal sacrifice. In the Bible, there is no better evidence of this transition than in the story of Abraham and Isaac in Genesis 22, where Abraham is told to spare his son and to offer in his place the ram that he will find in the brush.

From a literary point of view, this is a magnificent narrative. The listeners know the outcome even as they hear the tale. From an artistic point, this tale has inspired some of the greatest works of Western art, including no small number of painting masterpieces and the incomparable Ghiberti bronze doors of the Florence baptistery.[1] The story of Abraham's sacrifice clearly spells out that the god of the Hebrews did not want a human blood sacrifice. The rejection of human blood sacrifice, as outlined in Genesis 22, suggests a significant development in human social evolution.

In the classical world we also find cases of human sacrifice.[2] The most outstanding myth of human sacrifice in the Greek world is that of Iphigenia,[3] a tale that mirrors that of Jephthah's Daughter in the Old Testament (Judges 11–12). Such tales date to our most ancient times. In the civilized West, as societies developed and matured, human sacrifice eventually ceased and was replaced by animal sacrifice. With the fall of the classical civilizations and the rise of Christianity, animal sacrifice also disappeared and was replaced by the ritual sacrifice of the Mass, a re-enactment of the human blood sacrifice of Calvary.

While the Protestant Reformation re-described the Catholic mass by insisting that the mass was not a re-enactment of Calvary since the sacrifice of Jesus was made only once and for all, the Protestant Churches still retain, perhaps even more than the Catholic, a deep sense of the Calvary blood sacrifice. Thus, through the repeated recollection of Jesus as a blood sacrifice, Christianity has returned its followers to the most primitive state of humankind.

We must ask, what is the source of the notion of Jesus as a blood sacrifice? According to Gospel accounts, Jesus himself never says a word about his death being a sacrifice to compensate for sin. While Jesus indeed tells his followers that he will be handed over to the authorities, there is no

---

[1] Michelangelo called these doors "The Gates of Paradise."
[2] It could be argued, however, that Roman gladiatorial games, at least in their origins, were human sacrifice.
[3] It must be noted that not all ancient Greek sources agree on her death. Some sources state that Iphigenia was carried away to safety by the gods.

mention as to why (Mark 9:30–32, Matthew 17:22–23, Matthew 20: 17–19). The gospels are silent on this notion.

To find our answer we must look at the epistles of Paul. Of the several Paul's attestations as to Jesus being a blood sacrifice, I note here but two. "But now in Christ Jesus, you who once were far off have been brought near by the blood of Christ" (Ephesians 2:13) and again, "The cup of blessing that we bless, is it not a participation in the blood of Christ?" (Corinthians 10:16). In this verse, the notion of a human blood sacrifice becomes all the more abhorrent. Is there any concept more savage than the notion that drinking the blood of a human sacrifice will imbue the participant with some kind of metaphysical power or sanctity?

In the epistle to the Hebrews, we find a most striking example human sacrifice replacing animal sacrifice: "He entered once for all into the Holy Place, taking not the blood of goats and calves but his own blood, thus securing an eternal redemption"(9:12).[1] Each of these references, whether by Paul or by someone who lived in Paul's time, illustrates the reversed notion of human blood replacing animal blood. Chapter 5 will devote itself to a full consideration of the notion of the crucifixion as the means of redemption.

The Second Question: Original Sin

The first fundamental question of a god who demands a blood sacrifice takes us to the second fundamental question: the doctrine of Original Sin, most succinctly summed up in the verse of the New England Primer of 1777, "In Adam's fall, we sinned all."

It is this "Fall" of our mythical ancestors Adam and Eve that initiates the Christian salvation story. This story, misread on the part of Paul, as we shall see in Chapter 4, culminates in the crucifixion and death of Jesus, a sacrifice that secures our redemption. Thus, the Fall merges with the crucifixion in an inextricable bond where one act is meaningless without the other. Without the Fall there is no need for the coming of Jesus to redeem humankind. The fall is, in the words of the Latin Easter prayer, the "felix culpa" the "happy fall" without which Jesus would not have come among us. Indeed, from this perspective the Fall is not a pointless event. It is necessary.

O certe necessarium Adamae peccatum	Oh, this necessary sin of Adam
Quod Christi morte deletum est	For which Christ was subject to death
O felix culpa	Oh, happy fall
Quae talem ac tantum meruit habere	For such as all to merit to have
Redemptorem	The Redeemer

---

[1] As we shall see in Chapter 5, Paul is not held to be the author of this epistle.

But there was no Adam and no Eve. That story is a wonderful myth. And if there was no "Adam and Eve," there was no Fall. There was no "Birth Sin" that we inherited. There was no "Original Sin," a term that was to be coined by Saint Augustine some four hundred years later. I would propose that most Western Christians,[1] Protestant or Catholic, do not know that the term "Original Sin" is found nowhere in the bible. While there is some debate as to the first use of the exact words "Original Sin," it is certainly Saint Augustine in the fifth century who fixes the concept in the doctrinal lexicon.[2]

During the Reformation it is John Calvin who seizes upon the Original Sin doctrine for fuel in his rantings. For Calvin, humankind is innately corrupt. We are born in sin.

> As Adam's spiritual life would have consisted in remaining united and bound to his Maker, so estrangement from him was the death of his soul..... This is the hereditary corruption to which early Christian writers gave the name of Original Sin, meaning by the term the depravation of a nature formerly good and pure.... We thus see that the impurity of parents is transmitted to their children, so that all, without exception, are originally depraved.[3]

How is it, we must ask, that we still accept if not the literal meaning of such words then the ramifications of their intent?

To find reference to the Fall itself, we turn to the book of Genesis, a topic we will explore in Chapter 4, where in the second creation story (2:4–3:24), Adam and Eve transgress God's command not to eat of the tree of the knowledge of good and evil.[4] Genesis, however, does not define that fall as a sin that must be redeemed.

In the second creation story, Adam and Eve are driven from the garden to suffer in the world, and that is the end of the tale. Furthermore, we find nothing else either in the Old Testament or in the gospels that suggests that the fall of Adam and Eve requires redemption.

Indeed, in none of the gospel accounts does Jesus ever mention the names of Adam and Eve or anything about their transgression. It would seem that the Jesus of the gospels does not know that he has been sent to redeem the sin of our first parents. It is not until the epistles of Paul, as we shall see in Chapter 5, that a connection is made between the transgression of "Adam" and the death of Jesus (Romans 5:14–19). Thus, once again, the principal

---

[1] I specify "Western" here because the Eastern Church refers to the fall as Ancestral Sin and has a different interpretation.

[2] See also Irenaeus of Lyon, *Against Heresies* V, 19.

[3] Edited from Book 2, Chapter 1, *The Institutes of The Christian Religion*, London Hatfield Edition, 1599

[4] As we will see in Chapter 4, the first creation story in Genesis describes not a "Fall" but a blessing.

spokesman for the idea of redemption from a fallen state goes to the same person who gave us the notion of the need for a blood sacrifice, Paul.

As mentioned in the consideration of our first question, few Christians stop to consider the implications of a blood sacrifice to a wrathful god. What is more, they have given little deep thought to examining the cause of that sacrifice and the need for redemption. If humankind needs redemption, redemption from what? A mythical sin? In Christian doctrine, the notion of the need for redemption implicitly involves the concept of humankind's transgression or fall at some primal state of our existence. Without the belief in some kind of "fall," there is no foundation for belief in a redemption.

Now, in traditional terms, the story of the "Fall" is represented in the second creation story of Genesis, a topic that we will explore at length in Chapter 4. Even for the contemporary, educated Christian who recognized the Genesis story as a metaphor and not a historical account, the germ of the myth is that mankind at some time corrupted his nature such that we needed to be redeemed. The idea of redemption from a fallen state goes the same person who gave us the notion of the need for a blood sacrifice, Paul.

The Third Question: Resurrection and Ascension

The doctrine of the resurrection from the dead is not only awkwardly devised on a scriptural basis but is a doctrine that confounds all rational understanding of the world we live in. The same Christian god who demands the blood of a human victim in compensation for the supposed transgression of humankind's progenitors will now, in recognition of that sacrifice, turn death back into life. Not only has this heretofore bloodthirsty (now turned compassionate) god restored the primary sacrificial victim, Jesus, but he will restore all humankind at some sublime moment in the future. The resurrection of Jesus as recounted in the gospels is hardly a consistent story, which is curious for a tale of such importance. The theology of the tale, however, relies less on the gospels than on the epistles of Paul who is the first to recount in writing the miracle of Jesus' resuscitation. "Now if Christ is preached as raised from the dead, how can some of you say that there is no resurrection of the dead?" (1 Corinthians 15:12). Thus, Paul sets out the fundamental theological notion and doctrine of the resurrection of the dead.

As with the notion of a blood-demanding god, the concept of some form of life after death dates from humankind's earliest beliefs. Ancient humans buried the dead with objects from life to serve the deceased in the next world. In ancient Egypt, the mummification of the body assured the continuation of life. In the East, notions of reincarnation assured the continuity of existence. The Greeks and Romans also had some notion of the transmigration of the soul, a "metempsychosis." While none of these practices or beliefs may have included a physical resurrection, they still express the need for the continuation of life in some form. We, as beings with an awareness of ourselves, cannot fully deal with the notion that the "self" may one day cease: that we will no longer be "aware." As Descartes noted in his most notable quotation, "I think therefore, I am." The one thing we cannot conceive of is our own non-being.[1]

The thought of our non-existence is far too troubling, far too isolating. Our non-existence is a thought that leaves us ultimately alone, abandoned and with no hope whatsoever. Thus, the thought of a resurrection from the dead is a most comforting, even though illogical, solution. In holding fast to the doctrine of the resurrection of the dead, Christians hold a religious belief completely isolated from the sphere of a logical and rational universe.

From a rational point we must ask: why is rising from the dead necessary? What does it fulfill in the scheme of the infinite universe? Why is it necessary to abort the process of nature, a nature supposedly created by a rational god, by taking what is dead and returning it to life? Such a restoration contradicts the very pattern of all existence: an existence that, in theory, this same god set in place. In other words, why create and then terminate, only to re-generate? If I, as a mere mortal, can see the pointless inefficiency of such a system, how is such a notion logical to the far greater intellect of a god?

Coupled with the doctrine of the resurrection is that the belief that the newly restored-body will then experience some kind of bodily ascension into heaven. What notion could be more impossible? In an infinite universe whose nature we cannot begin to comprehend, where is that place to which the physical human body will ascend? To the ancient world where the gods lived in material abode somewhere above the ethers, such an ascent was possible. We, however, live with the knowledge of a very different universe. There is no heavenly sphere, no empyrean, no Olympus. We live in a world whose science has offered sophisticated mirror and radio telescopes, and even these devices cannot begin to fathom the extent of an ever expanding universe. The notion of a "heaven above" to which a physical body ascends to dwell for eternity is without reason. Does today's Christian take a moment to think through the belief in resurrection and ascension, in the context of what we know of the universe?

Has today's Christian compared physical reality to the myths of wishful thinking that cloud our perceptions? The doctrines of the Resurrection and Ascension will be our subject in Chapter 7.

---

[1] "Then, I examined with care what I was, and seeing that I could suppose that I had no body, and that there was no world nor any place in which I might be; but that I could not for that reason, suppose that I was not." *Discourse On the Method, Part IV*

The Fourth Question: Who Was Jesus and What Did He Teach?

In Chapter 7 *Reason and Doctrine* will examine two points about Jesus himself: what did Jesus really teach and who did he think he was? For these two points we will rely heavily of scripture. Did Jesus really teach a message of love? If so, why is it that in the oldest gospel, that of Mark, he uses the word "love" only once? Why does Mark's Jesus never teach the Lord's Prayer or preach the Sermon on the Mount? How is it that the notion of love for one's fellows develops not from a concept found in all the gospels but as a notion that develops only gradually? Why is it that John's gospel, written well after the other three, is riddled with love sayings as compared to the synoptic gospels? We again come to the epistles of Paul, where we ask how much of the love message is due to Jesus and how much is due to Paul.

Chapter 8 will then chance a brief foray into speculation. Who was Jesus? What might we understand from his very name? What is the significance of the word "Jesus," when we consider that in Aramaic the name means "savior"?

We then look more closely at the appellation "Messiah," that is, "anointed (king)." When taken together in their original meanings, the words suggest a different picture of the preacher from Galilee. What was Jesus' idea of himself? Did he really think he was to be the promised king of Israel? After all, we are told he made a great public display upon his entrance into Jerusalem where the people called him "son of David," a title clearly indicative of kingship. Who were Jesus' followers and what did they expect of him, and what did they expect for themselves?

Furthermore, as all four gospels attest, Jesus' followers were armed. Did Jesus' belief and that of his followers in the notion that he would be king lead to his execution for very valid political reasons?

The Fifth Question: Can Christianity Survive without Doctrine?

Chapter 10 will restate the distinction made in this book between Christian doctrine and Christian teaching. While we must reject Christian doctrine as an offense against all reason, it is my hope that we may maintain the cultural and social values of Christian teachings.

Can we raise our consciousness and cast aside the superstition of blood thirsty gods, sacrificial victims and imaginary resurrections and live for the values of concern and respect for one another and for the world in which we live?

Chapter 2. Establishing a Ground Work: Scripture

Before engaging the complex interconnections of the questions this book presents, I think it necessary to establish an overview of my reading and interpretation of scripture. Let me establish from the beginning my certainty that the scriptures are clearly not inerrant.[1] They are not the inspired word of God. The scriptures are the fabrication of human authors that detail myth and invention mixed with a modicum of possible history. They are not texts produced at a single moment of spiritual inspiration but were created over hundreds of years and most were written well after the times they describe.

The foundation of all Judeo-Christian belief derives from that collection of works we call the Bible, probably the most used and abused text in the history of mankind. From a language point of view, the word "bible" simply means "book," from the Greek, "biblia" (βιβλία). The term "bible," or rather the Greek βιβλία, originally referred to the scrolls on which the text was written. There is nothing sacred or mystical in the word. The word "bible" was not handed down by divine revelation.

In the Christian world the Bible is divided into two portions. The first portion that Christians call The Old Testament and Jews call the Tanakh contains material composed prior to the life of Jesus of Nazareth. The first section of the Tanakh, the Torah, is a compilation of five books that, by tradition, were written by the hand of Moses: Genesis, Exodus, Leviticus, Deuteronomy and Numbers. Contemporary scholarship, however, clearly indicates that the five books are a compilation of several sources merged as a single text.

---

[1] See the works of Bart D. Ehrman for a close study of the history and evolution of scripture.

The Old Testament as we know it was not composed at a single time. The stories are a collection of texts set in writing by different people at distinct points in history. Many scholars assign the writing to four distinct groups. The first of the four is the "Yahwists" whose name for God was the tetragrammaton, "YHWH." Their stories may date as early as the 900s BC. Following their writings are the "Elohists," whose name for God was Elohim. Their accounts date from about 100 years later. The third group is the "Deuteronomical," whose writings were composed yet another hundred years later.

In much current biblical scholarship, these four groups are labeled respectively, "P" (Priestly), "E" (Elohist), and "Y" (Yahwist) and "D" Deuteronomical. These tales were collected and organized sometime in the 7th century before the Christian era. This was the time when the Hebrews were permitted to return to Israel from Babylon after their "captivity" there. The collating of the texts was carried out by what scholars call the "priestly" group. It was they who edited and strung together the various accounts of the Torah in an attempt to create the impression of a cohesive narrative. The texts that they edited were for the most part earlier tales created by the other three groups. Indeed, there are some scholars who see this moment of the final text assembly as the start of the nation of Israel.

Many of the stories in Genesis and the other texts are found in multiple versions, each with slight or even significant variations. As noted, one of the key indicators that signal the hand of a different author or source is the word that the writer uses for "god." When, for example, we read the simple title "God," in Hebrew this is usually denoted as El or Elohim.[1] Since we find this term in the first chapter of Genesis, we know we are reading the works of an "Elohistic" compiler. When, however, we read in English "Lord God," (in Hebrew Yahweh[2] Elohim), as we do in the second chapter of Genesis, the writing is the work of a different school of editing, often referred to as the "Yahwistic" tradition. There cannot be any doubt that the two accounts derive from very distinct and very different sources.

Just as the use of a plural noun "Elohim" is the subject of much study, so too the second tale's use of "Yahweh" generates many questions. The exact meaning of "Yahweh" is a question for linguistic scholars who still ponder the word's origins. It seems that most scholars agree that the word is the Tetragrammaton, the four letters YHWH. Some research suggests that the

---

[1] Much ink has been expended in an effort to explain this plural. Does it reflect a very primitive notion of a multiple godhead, or perhaps even a god and his consort? Or, as many would like it, is this simply something of a royal "we?" I leave this question to experts in the field.

[2] Sometimes transcribed as YHVH.

letters YHWH are related to the verb "to be." [1] The term "Yahweh" is often translated simply as "Lord God." To my knowledge there is no substantial reason for this translation. From my knowledge of the name and word "YHWH," there is nothing that suggests that "YHWH" means "Lord God." Be that as it may, for our purposes the point is that there is a distinction between the god "Elohim" and the god "Yahweh." These are two distinct deities whose creation myths are equally distinct.

Thus, as we said, there are at least two schools or traditions that, at some point, probably around the ninth century before the time of Jesus, sewed together the two traditions into a less than seamless narrative. The careful reader can easily distinguish the difference between the two versions. Evidence for sewing together of the two traditions is easily found even by the casual reader's exploration of the Torah.

In addition to the two versions of the Creation story, there is the Flood story which most people think they know. Most people, however, probably do not. In Genesis 6, the god "Elohim" commands that two of each animal be brought on board the ark, "Of the birds according to their kinds, and of the animals according to their kinds, of every creeping thing of the ground according to its kind, two of every sort shall come in to you, to keep them alive" (6:20). But, in Genesis 7, Noah's god is "Yahweh." Moreover, strange to tell, and little known by most people, this god demands that fourteen of each animal be brought aboard.

> Take with you seven pairs of all clean animals, the male and his mate; and a pair of the animals that are not clean, the male and his mate;[2] and seven pairs of the birds of the air also, male and female, to keep their kind alive upon the face of all the earth (7:2–3).

The flood story in the book of Genesis is not the only example of the distinct use of these two names. Doublings of this kind are common in Genesis. Compare the story of Abraham and Abimelech (Genesis 20) where god is Elohim with Isaac and Abimelech where god is Yahweh (Genesis 26). More to our point are the two distinct creation stories in Genesis, one of which will serve as the foundation of one of the most irrational Christian doctrines, the doctrine of humankind's Fall from grace and its subsequent doctrines of redemption and resurrection. We will hold the full discussion of the Genesis problem until Chapter 4.

And Genesis is not the only book with multiple accounts of a single story that have been merged as one. The book of Exodus, for example, sets out

---

[1] Older English translations like the King James Version often use "Jehovah."
[2] A curious point in this account: if god was cleansing the world of sin, why would he want to save the "unclean" animals? Of course, we might also ask why he created them in the first place.

two distinct regulations for the observance of Passover. Chapter 12 verses 1–11 determine the slaughter of a lamb as the foundation of the feast. Verses 12–20, however, set out the rules for the eating of unleavened bread as the focal element of the Passover festival to be recalled each year. The two rituals as described in Exodus have nothing in common. They have simply been placed side by side by a scribe in antiquity. The scribe clearly took them from independent sources and collated them. The difference between the two ordinances may be somewhat difficult to distinguish but they are clearly there for the observant reader. Here again, tradition and habit have blinded our perception and confused what we think a text may say and what the text itself is actually telling us.

In the books that follow Genesis and Exodus, there are likewise numerous discrepancies. After the Torah come the remaining books of the Old Testament, called collectively in Hebrew the Tanakh. "Tanakh" is an acronym for the full collection. The acronym is comprised of the "T" of Torah, the first five books, [1] the "N" of Nevi'im, the Prophets, and the "K" of Ketuvim, the Writings. The texts that follow the Torah are books of the history of the Jewish people in Israel and Judah, the stories of Saul and David and Solomon, the stories of the prophets and the stories of heroes like the Maccabees, Daniel, Esther and Susanna. There are also books of great poetry like the Psalms and the Song of Songs. There are books of admonition and hope featuring the prophets like Isaiah and Jeremiah. We even find great theater, equal to that of the Greeks, in the book of Job. Moreover, the tribulations and intrigues of the house of David are every bit as dramatic as the trials of the house of Atreus and the conflicts of Agamemnon. Take, for example, a scene from the revolt of David's son, Absalom. "So they pitched a tent for Absalom upon the roof [of the palace] and Absalom went in to his father's concubines in the sight of all of Israel" (2 Samuel 16:22). What tale could be more salacious?

Differences and contradictions are not limited to Genesis and Exodus. To cite them all would be a study unto itself. For the sake of simple illustration, I will point out but a few. In 1 Samuel, Saul takes his own life and dies on his sword along with his bodyguard. "Then Saul said to his armor-bearer, "Draw your sword, and thrust me through with it, lest these uncircumcised come and thrust me through, and make sport of me." But his armor-bearer would not; for he feared greatly. Therefore Saul took his own sword, and fell upon it" (1 Samuel 31).

At the beginning of 2 Samuel, however, the text tells us that Saul did not die from his own sword but required the final hand of a soldier: "So I stood

---

[1] The Torah, tradition says, was composed by Moses. This of course can hardly be the case.

beside him, and slew him, because I was sure that he could not live after he had fallen; and I took the crown which was on his head and the armlet which was on his arm, and I have brought them here to my lord" (2 Samuel 1).

Many fundamentalist scripture experts may offer rationalizations of these two accounts in some kind of contrived synthesis, but they are clearly two different stories that do not agree. Dissimilarities are discernible in other places. The accounts of how David came into the service of Saul are several. In 1 Samuel 16, David goes to Saul's court to play the harp for him. At the beginning of chapter 17, Saul gives David his own armor to protect the young man in his upcoming battle with Goliath. Yet, by the end of the chapter, Saul does not seem to know who the young man is who killed the giant. There can be no doubt that these various versions are taken from different traditions and that they have been sewn together to create some kind of attempted uniform—if somewhat illogical—whole. Indeed, we might well ask who actually killed Goliath. We all know the "David" story, but 2 Samuel 21:19 tells us, "And there was again war with the Philistines at Gob; and Elhanan the son of Jaareoregim, the Bethlehemite, slew Goliath the Gittite, the shaft of whose spear was like a weaver's beam."[1] So, who killed Goliath? But let us now consider the New Testament.

The New Testament is composed of twenty-seven individual books that have as their common point a certain Jesus, said to be of the town of Nazareth. All of the books of the New Testament including the gospels that claim to narrate his life were composed well after the death of Jesus. It would be incomplete to consider the accepted books of the New Testament as the only works from ancient times that tell of Jesus. Indeed, the texts of the New Testament as we now know them are but a small representation of the texts about Jesus that proliferated the early centuries of Christianity. The full investigation into these extra-canonical writings is an ongoing study to which much attention has already been given by many biblical scholars.[2] The number of texts written about Jesus will probably never be known. Many have either been deliberately destroyed or have been simply lost to time.

---

[1] For full academic honesty I must note that 1 Chronicles 20:5 amends the victim to become the brother of Goliath.

[2] See for example. *The Other Bible*, Barnstone, Willis, editor. For a most charming tale, read *The Infancy Gospel of Thomas*. I excerpt here. "And a certain Jew when he saw what Jesus did, playing upon the Sabbath day, departed straightway and told his father Joseph: Lo, thy child is at the brook, and he hath taken clay and fashioned twelve little birds, and hath polluted the Sabbath day. And Joseph came to the place and saw: and cried out to him, saying: Wherefore doest thou these things on the Sabbath, which it is not lawful to do? But Jesus clapped his hands together and cried out to the sparrows and said to them: Go! and the sparrows took their flight and went away chirping. And when the Jews saw it they were amazed, and departed and told their chief men that which they had seen Jesus do."

Some have survived to this day in various forms and fragments that have been recently discovered.[1]

The four gospels in our New Testament were selected by Irenaeus of Lyon at the end of the second century, on the basis of a peculiar logic. Irenaeus writes,

> The heretics boast that they have many more gospels than there really are. But really they don't have any gospels that aren't full of blasphemy. There actually are only four authentic gospels. And this is obviously true because there are four corners of the universe and there are four principal winds, and therefore there can be only four gospels that are authentic. These, besides, are written by Jesus' true followers.[2]

The date when the entire collection of texts, gospels, epistles, Revelation and Acts was accepted depends on whether one follows the Roman Catholic list or the Protestant selection. Most of the texts as we now know them were established as valid by various councils that issued various edicts at various times. It was not until 1546 that the Roman Council of Trent codified its books of the New Testament. The Church of England sets up its canon in 1563, and the King James Bible appears in 1611.

The oldest of the New Testament texts are the seven authentic epistles of Paul: First Thessalonians, Philippians, Philemon, First Corinthians, Galatians, Second Corinthians and Romans. These epistles are considered by scholars to have been written somewhere between the years 50 and 60.[3] Of course, at the time of their writing, no one thought of them as texts to be included in the collection that would become the New Testament. We will examine Paul's writing in Chapter 5.

The first three gospels (Matthew, Mark and Luke) are called the Synoptics, from the Greek "syn – opticos," meaning "the same sight," or, from the same point of view. As the designation "synoptic" suggests, these three texts are often quite similar in content. Some scholars, perhaps most, believe that the similarities of these texts results from a kind of synthesis between the gospel of Mark and an older source, now lost. German specialists were

---

[1] See, for example, the findings at Nag Hammadi in 1945.

[2] Irenaeus also writes: "It is not possible that the Gospels can be either more or fewer in number than they are. For, since there are four zones of the world in which we live, and four principal winds, while the Church is scattered throughout all the world, and the pillar and ground of the Church is the Gospel and the spirit of life; it is fitting that she should have four pillars, breathing out immortality on every side, and vivifying men afresh. From which fact, it is evident that the Word, the Artificer of all, He that sits upon the cherubim, and contains all things, He who was manifested to men, has given us the Gospel under four aspects, but bound together by one Spirit" (Against Heresies, 3:11:8.)

[3] 1 Timothy, 2 Timothy and Titus are generally considered by most scholars as written by another author, later. Ephesians, Colossians, 2 Thessalonians are held as uncertain.

the first to look into this deeply, and they referred to the lost work as "Q," from the German word "quelle" ("source"). That name was picked up and is now commonly used to designate the presumed lost book. Another possibility proposes that there is no "Q" but that Matthew and Luke are based on Mark alone. Of course, as with much of New Testament scholarship, the history and derivation of the synoptics are still being debated. Even so, while the general outline of these three synoptic gospels can be aligned in great measure, there remain characteristics distinct to each that allow each gospel to be identified in its own right. The Jesus of each is presented in very distinguishable ways. The attuned reader or listener at a Sunday gospel reading can readily discern one gospel narrator from the other.

Of all the gospels, Mark is generally considered the oldest. It may date from as early as the year 50, but most scholars set its composition somewhere between 60 and 70. Mark is also the simplest of the accounts. Mark, for example, stresses the coming of a new kingdom but mentions neither the Lord's Prayer nor the Sermon on the Mount. Mark seems to know nothing of virginal conceptions or miraculous births. Mark's Jesus is concerned about his public image and speaks secretively about those who understand and those who do not understand his message. Mark's Jesus concentrates much on casting out demons, has little to say on the topic of brotherly love, and a great deal to say about the imminent arrival of a new kingdom. He never mentions the beatitudes ("Blessed are they who...."); and he does not seem to know the "Lord's Prayer." Even the original conclusion of Mark's gospel mentions nothing of the "Great Commission" to teach all nations (16:15). Nor does it include the ascension of Jesus into heaven (16:19). Most biblical scholars affirm that the concluding verses of Mark from 16:9 to 16:20 were a later addition. [1]

The Gospel of Matthew takes the reader into a decidedly different realm with a decidedly different Jesus. In the first place, most scholarship holds that Matthew's gospel, unlike any of the others, was written by a Jewish author with a Jewish audience in mind. One indication of his Jewish background is that Matthew seems to understand the meaning of the name Jesus in Hebrew as "savior," a fine point not mentioned by the other evangelists (Matthew 1:21).[2] While nowhere in Matthew does Jesus actually claim to be divine, Matthew embellishes his Jesus story with various elements to suggest it. In Matthew, Jesus is born of divine sources. His Jesus is visited by the Magi who recognize him as a king. Like Moses, the Jesus of Matthew is the cause of an infant massacre and like Moses he comes out of Egypt (Matthew 2). Unlike Mark's Jesus, Matthew's Jesus gives us the Sermon on the Mount

---

[1] See the note in the RSV and also in other translations concerning the later addition of these verses.

[2] See Chapter 8.

(Matthew 5) and knows the "Lord's Prayer" (Matthew 6). But, Matthew's Jesus makes no celestial ascent, and in that he matches up with the original ending of the book of Mark. Matthew's Jesus simply ends with the "Great Commission."[1]

The third of the synoptics is the gospel of Luke. Luke is a brilliant story teller. Of all the gospels, Luke is the most literary. His tale of Jesus is a solidly constructed narrative embellished with great creativity and invention. In Luke, the attuned reader appreciates not only what is said but the way it is said. This is a gospel of solid craftsmanship. We might take as an example the way Luke lines up the time sequences in his narrative. Note how, in the following example, he moves in the opening chapters from event to event and interweaves them to create a narrative whole. Luke begins his narrative not with Jesus but with the foretelling of John the Baptist's birth. Only then does he change scenes in a kind of "meanwhile, back at the ranch" device, where he introduces the announcement of the birth of Jesus—the annunciation. From there we read of Mary's visit to Elizabeth. At this point Luke joins not only the foretelling of the two births but also the fact that they are cousins. The sequence then ends with the birth of John the Baptist, which is mirrored and culminated in the birth of Jesus. Luke's sequencing of the events is quite remarkable. This is certainly not a narrative that has been compiled haphazardly.

Luke's gospel, written after Mark and Matthew, is also clearly influenced by what must have been the gradual accretion of social and theological ideas in the evolving Christian movement. It is in the gospel of Luke alone, for example, that we find some of the most memorable parables of Jesus: parables that stand as the highest examples of Christian care and concern for others. It is Luke who tells of the Prodigal Son (15: 11–32), the Lost Drachma (15:8–10), the Lost Sheep (15:1–7) and perhaps the most famous of all, a story whose very name is part of common vocabulary, The Good Samaritan (10:29–37). We will discuss these parables further in Chapter 7, "What Did Jesus Teach?"

Not only do most Christian merge the various Jesus images into one image, they often hybridize the tales. The most evident example of this kind of hybridization is the nativity story. Few Christians realize that neither Mark nor John relates the birth of Jesus. In fact, these two authors are at polar opposites as to the origins of their Jesus. To relate the story as we know it, you must take passages from both Matthew and Luke, each of whom has a different tale.

---

[1] One has to wonder what became of Matthew's Jesus after he rose from the dead.

Matthew gives us angels and shepherds. Luke gives us the Magi. Other elements of the Nativity account are direct adaptations from the Old Testament. Matthew's slaughter of the Innocents (Matthew 2: 13–23), for example, mirrors Pharaoh's decree to drown the first born of Israel (Exodus 1:22). Details in Luke's account of the annunciation and the incarnation of Jesus recall the story of Hannah in the book of First Samuel. Mary's "Magnificat" in Luke (1: 46–55) is a direct take from the Song of Hannah (1 Samuel 2: 1–10). Compare Hannah's song, "My heart exults in the Lord; my strength is exalted in the Lord. My mouth derides my enemies, because I rejoice in thy salvation" with Mary's "Magnificat": And Mary said, "My soul magnifies the Lord, and my spirit rejoices in God my Savior, for he has regarded the low estate of his handmaiden. For behold, henceforth all generations will call me blessed."

Yet, most Christians are oblivious to these points and unconsciously take what they have been told or what they think they know and merge together a polyphony of influences and sources without a moment of thought to examine the source material individually.

One of the most salient discrepancies that most Christians overlook, despite the fact that they have heard the multiple versions their entire lives, are the various accounts of the resurrection of Jesus. None of the four gospels agree on this phenomenon in any way. In addition to the multiple resurrection tales, we must consider the accounts of the crucifixion itself. In John, Jesus does not even die on the same day as the Jesus of the other three gospels.

These are but a few samples. The New Testaments is riddled with many more. If the bible is inerrant, how does one account for such a variety of accounts detailing the same event? Let us leave the synoptics and turn to the most complex gospel, that of John. John's gospel was the latest of the New Testament texts to be written, and it may well date from around the year 90 or 95, some sixty years after the time of the Jesus it proposes to describe. While John, too, deals with Jesus, his Jesus is not the simple itinerant Jewish preacher and wonderworker of the Synoptics. John does not concern himself with the populist appeal of a Sermon on the Mount or a "Lord's Prayer." The Jesus John intends to illustrate is nothing short of a mystical sage whose words and deeds are loaded with philosophical and theological implications. The gospel of John is a work of metaphysics with Jesus as the enlightened sage. Anyone with an attentive knowledge of John will immediately recognize his Hellenistic bent for the philosophical. The opening verses of his gospel, "In the beginning was the word and the word was with God and the word was God," immediately tell us that we dealing with a very different point of view. Even the miracles of Jesus in John's writings take on a highly metaphorical quality. John's Jesus changes "water into wine" (John 2), and he raises from his tomb a man who has been dead for four days (John 11). Such miracles, had they truly happened, would certainly not have been forgotten or omitted by the earlier authors, yet, no other gospels even hint at such events.

Miracles such as these are the distinct imaginative property of John. The stories, while usually taken literally, are clearly metaphorical. Changing water into wine is the changing of the mundane into the divine. Raising the dead to life is what attending to the teachings of Jesus will achieve spiritually.

The most important metaphor in John is also one of the most important differences between John and the Synoptics. It is John's account of the passion. In recounting the passion, John does not follow the sequence of the Synoptics where Jesus shares the Passover supper with his disciples on the night before his execution. In John, the dates are shifted such that Jesus shares his Last Supper not on Passover but on the night *before* the Passover. In this way John can have his Jesus be crucified on the very Passover day. By shifting that date, John's Jesus replaces the Passover lamb: Jesus becomes the victim, the *new* Passover.

As with the changing of the water into wine, John revels in the creation of philosophical metaphor. Probably the cleverest use of metaphor in John is set out rather interestingly in the story of the "Woman at the Well," another story found only in John and one where most listeners are quite unable to grasp its subtleties.

> He had to pass through Samaria. So he came to a city of Samaria, called Sychar, near the field that Jacob gave to his son Joseph. Jacob's well was there, and so Jesus, wearied as he was with his journey, sat down beside the well. It was about the sixth hour. There came a woman of Samaria to draw water. Jesus said to her, "Give me a drink." The Samaritan woman said to him, "How is it that you, a Jew, ask a drink of me, a woman of Samaria?" For Jews have no dealings with Samaritans. For his disciples had gone away into the city to buy food. Jesus answered her, "If you knew the gift of God, and who it is that is saying to you, 'Give me a drink,' you would have asked him, and he would have given you living water. Are you greater than our father Jacob, who gave us the well, and drank from it himself, and his sons, and his cattle?" Jesus said to her, "Everyone who drinks of this water will thirst again, but whoever drinks of the water that I shall give him will never thirst; the water that I shall give him will become in him a spring of water welling up to eternal life." The woman said to him, "Sir, give me this water, that I may not thirst, nor come here to draw."
> (John 4:3–15)

As we can see, the tale of the woman at the well itself is a metaphor: a metaphor about the nature of metaphors. It is nothing short of a brilliant construction to demonstrate a point. In this tale, Jesus wants to offer the woman the metaphoric water that will leave its recipient quenched and never thirsty again. The woman, however, cannot grasp the concept of a metaphor. She can only think in concrete terms. She is looking for real, physical water. Real water, however, is not what Jesus offers. In this wonderfully crafted scene, John's Jesus is offering the metaphysical water of eternal life. Of course, as with most of the tales in John, this little account is found in no other gospel. The tale of the woman at the well is quintessential John. No other gospel writer contrives such metaphysical scenarios. The event at the well is clearly not history, for as the story tells us there are some who can grasp the abstract meaning of metaphor and others who can only deal with the concrete and literal.

Following the four gospels, the New Testament presents the single work "The Acts of the Apostles," a volume that is intended as an historical account of the events that occurred among the followers of Jesus immediately after his death. The author of this narrative is traditionally believed to be Luke, the same as the author of the gospel. Like Luke's gospel, this is an interestingly crafted tale with fascinating details and inventions. While the text may not be overly rich in doctrinal foundations, it is a most interesting account of the vicissitudes of sea and land travel in the Roman world.

The next substantial division of texts is called the Epistles. The Epistles, twenty-one in number, are a series of letters allegedly composed by various followers of Jesus and addressed to various new Christian communities. These letters intend to offer guidelines to new converts on ways to conduct themselves as Christians and to function as a community. The Epistles themselves are divided into two main categories: those letters supposedly written by individuals who actually knew Jesus, such as James, Peter and Jude, and those letters from the most singular Paul of Tarsus, who, by his own admission, never knew Jesus during his lifetime. It is the letters of Paul that are of significant interest. We shall treat them in their own chapter.

The twenty-one epistles are followed by the final book of the New Testament, that infinite source of doom and gloom, that favorite text of fire-and-brimstone preachers who are ever ready to proclaim the ultimate script of worldly destruction: the Apocalypse, or The Book of Revelations.

The validity of this text as an account that derives from true apostolic sources has often been a topic of discussion. (Luther, for one, did not think Revelations should be accepted within the canon of the New Testament.[1]) It is not our purpose here to consider that text. Its visions and prophecies tell us little, if anything, about the development of doctrine that is our interest, but it must be said that Revelations as a fully-charged illustration of the

---

[1] *Preface to the Revelation of Saint John*, 1522.

"End Times" offers something of a dramatic conclusion to the bible as a whole and provides a seemingly never ending source of material for everyone from artists to musicians, writers, filmmakers and of course, televangelists. And so, with this cataclysmic *finale*, we have the twenty-seven books of the New Testament and the last word of a thousand-year saga that started out in Genesis with the phrase "In the beginning."

When we look at its history objectively, it is clear that what we call the Bible did not appear as a static, single and immutable arrangement of books. It was not "handed down" as a single text, as no small number of fundamentalists would contend. The contents of the bible have evolved over time, and what we now accept as a single compilation was only agreed upon well after the books were written. The books that the bible contains are not a divinely administered compilation but have been specifically selected by human intervention at given times in history to present the theology and politics of the compilers' own intents and inventions. Furthermore, when it comes to the New Testament, it has long been known that none of the texts that comprise it was written during the lifetime of Jesus, the person they claim to represent. These books, as wonderful a tale as they each may tell, are the compositions of skilled and often talented writers whose inspiration was, primarily, their own imagination. Here too, the accounts of the New Testament developed from a combination of certain possible historical incidents and willful personal agendas.

When we reflect on the New Testament as it has come down to us from Irenaeus, there is one striking observation. Most Christians do not consider the various accounts of the gospels and the epistles individually. They do not see the multiple faces of the principal character, Jesus, in each of the gospels and epistles as distinct creations. Most Christians tend to blend all the individual faces of Jesus into one. The confluence of texts overwhelms, subsumes and reshapes Christian doctrines to a certain preconceived conformity that these books individually do not contain. The merging of these texts further confuses the Christian mind already befuddled by habit and tradition. This merging of the various gospels inhibits any possible rational evaluation of the text as text.

The discussion of what constitutes the Bible is only touched upon in this chapter. The complexities of text establishment are a realm that demands the exploration of those who devote their lives to the study of textual criticism. What I have set out in this chapter is my understanding of the simple basics on the history of the bible in order to establish my point of departure for the chapters that follow. For a most thought-provoking and insightful study of this discipline, I would immediately turn the general public reader to the works of Bart D. Ehrman, particularly his *Misquoting Jesus* and *Jesus Interrupted*.

If you think you know the Bible and are most certain of the inerrancy of its words, Dr. Ehrman's studies will soon disabuse the critical and honest thinker who is willing to apply reason to the unquestioned habit of former misconceptions.

Chapter 3. Paul: "A Servant Set Apart"

To recapitulate Chapter 2, we recall that the scriptures, the Old and New Testaments, are the primary sources of Christian doctrine. Within these two volumes, however, there are certain books that seem to have a greater influence on doctrinal Christianity than do others. The Old Testament, as the parent document to the New, is the germinal source of the most significant of Christian doctrines. In the Old Testament we find Paul's groundwork for what would become the doctrine of Original Sin. New Testament writers make frequent use of selected passages from the Old Testament, often cited out of context, to substantiate their various notions on the nature and purpose of their individual Jesus. As mentioned in Chapter 2, the Jesus of each gospel is quite distinct. When we turn to the epistles, particularly those of Paul, we find yet another Jesus whose portrait is painted from an entirely different (if not even imaginatively contrived) perspective. In Paul, we discover not the *Jesus* of possible history as portrayed in the gospels but the invented *Christ* of salvation and resurrection without whom there is no redemption. Paul's Christ, like Paul himself, is a creation "set apart."

Our first point of consideration when reading Paul is his chronology in the New Testament. The portrait Paul paints of Jesus predates the individually distinct four images of Jesus found in the gospels. When viewed from the way the New Testament is composed, Paul's Jesus appears at first glance to be a fifth Jesus. In fact, however, Paul's Jesus may very well be the first and oldest Jesus, at least in literary terms. It is Paul's Jesus, a Jesus that Paul never knew, who may be the most influential in shaping the Jesus of the four gospels, all of which were written at later dates. The degree to which Paul's epistles influenced the authors of the four gospels is probably best left to the considerations of profession biblical scholars. Even so, I do think that Paul's overall view of Jesus was reflected in the writings of the evangelists, if not so much in Mark, then certainly by the time of Luke and John.

Who is the Jesus that Paul creates? Clearly even a cursory reading of the New Testament will reveal that Paul's Jesus is most distinct. Paul creates not only the sacrificial Jesus but the resurrected Jesus. To appreciate the distinct Jesus that Paul has invented, we have to do a little side stepping to the gospel of Mark. Even though Mark's gospel was written after Paul's epistles, the early date of its composition and the simplicity with which Mark narrates his tale may be a way to establish a base-line Jesus. Of the four gospels, Mark's Jesus seems to be the least influenced by the Jesus of Paul. While I can provide no incontrovertible evidence, the lack of the Pauline overtones may be because at the time of Mark's composition, Paul's teachings were still in their early stages. If we take Mark as our comparison to Paul, we quickly see the striking differences.

Mark's Jesus is a simple wandering preacher and healer who seems to know neither the Beatitudes nor the Lord's Prayer. He makes no claims of divinity and he seems to be taken with the notion that he is indeed the promised messiah king. Mark's Jesus has no miraculous conception at the word of an angel, and Mark's Jesus in the earliest manuscripts has no resurrection or ascension. In fact, the last the reader knows of Mark's Jesus is an empty tomb.

This Jesus is in marked contrast to Paul's god-selected human sacrifice to expiate the sins of all humankind. Mark's Jesus, with clearly little influence from Paul, speaks of love only once (Mark 12:30–33), when he quotes Leviticus 19:18. On the other hand, for the Jesus of Paul, love is the keyword. The Jesus of Paul and the Jesus of Mark are quite different. The differences and the influence of Paul become all the more apparent when we examine the development of the Jesus message as related by Matthew and Luke and especially by the last gospel, that of John. By the time the books of Matthew and Luke were composed, Paul's Jesus would possibly have been more influential. By the time of John's gospel, a good generation after Paul, the Jesus of John has surpassed Paul in the high theology of salvation and the notion of love for one's neighbor.

We now ask how did Paul develop the love message and attribute it to his Jesus? Was he influenced by certain Hellenistic philosophies or religions of his time? Was Paul's Jesus his own personal invention derived from some inner need or as a reaction to the state of society at the time? There seems to be no conclusive answer to the question. What we do know, however, and what is most curious about the influence of Paul, is that Paul himself never claims to have known Jesus. What Paul writes in his epistles is not what he heard from the mouth of Jesus, but rather he contends that "...we impart this in words not taught by human wisdom but taught by the Spirit, interpreting spiritual truths to those who possess the Spirit" (1 Corinthians 2:13). Yet, despite his lack of direct knowledge of Jesus, Paul is, among all the New Testament, the most vociferous in his proclamation of who and what Jesus was. Paul is not merely content to recast the minds of his fellow Jews but is entirely committed to the evangelization of the empire. Paul writes, "Now I am speaking to you Gentiles. Inasmuch then as I am an apostle to the Gentiles, I magnify my ministry in order to make my fellow Jews jealous and thus save some of them" (Romans 11: 13–14). But it is not only to the ancient empire of Rome that Paul speaks. Paul is the voice that will be heard for two thousand years to come. It is Paul to whom the following ages turn for their definition of the religion that will be called Christianity.

How did this man who presented himself as an ardent Jew and who claimed the privilege of Roman citizenship work his way into the role of the foremost disciple of Jesus? If Paul, as we understand from what he does not say in his epistles, did not know Jesus, what then is the source of Paul's work? How did he become such an authority on the teachings of Jesus? Unless, of course, Paul invented them. Now, at this point, a carefully prepared scholarly investigation would indeed be required if we are to better understand Paul's motivation. Nonetheless, Paul's writings, as the average person reads them, should offer some insight. For such a reading I would restate the premise of this book that the essential requirement for an honest evaluation of Christian doctrine is nothing more than properly applied common sense. When we properly apply common sense, as Descartes suggests, we cannot help but find Paul's involvement with members of the "The Way"[1] (as Acts tells us that Christians were first known) is nothing short of puzzling. Let us begin with the accounts of Paul's conversion.

The traditional and most commonly known story of Paul's conversion is found in The Acts of the Apostles, chapter 9, where Paul, on his way to the city of Damascus, is thrown from his horse and struck blind by a bolt of light. While this tale is certainly the best known account of Paul's transformation from persecutor of Christians to their most fanatical advocate it is not the only account of Paul's conversion. Outside the book of Acts, Paul himself, in his epistles, gives at least three other accounts, each completely different from the others. More important, none of them mentions the "road to Damascus" story. In fact, nowhere in Paul's writings does he seem to know that he was converted by being struck from a horse by a bolt of light. Does it not occur to today's Christian, reading Paul's works, that Paul himself never refers to

---

[1] Acts 9:2 "...so that if he [Paul] found any belonging to the Way, men or women, he might bring them bound to Jerusalem." See also Acts 24:14.

such a personally shattering event? There is no sign of such an event in Paul's epistles. Perhaps Paul does not mention the Damascus Road conversion because he would find it a far too banal encounter with the divine.[1]

Caravaggio, On the Road to Damascus, 1601

We will return to the traditional Damascus Road conversion tale at the conclusion of this chapter. We turn now instead to Paul's own words on how he was brought to his new faith.

For Paul, it would seem that his conversion was due to nothing as common as a fall from a horse. For Paul, in various versions that he tells, his conversion was far more metaphysical. According to his own words, Jesus came to him not in a physical bolt of light but rather in an intellectual illumination. Paul related his own various accounts of his conversion in his epistles but he never says a word about the Damascus road. The objective reader would have to ask how such an oversight on the part of the principal actor would be possible.[2] Following what is understood to be the chronology of Paul's epistles, we will move from 1 Corinthians to Galatians and then to 2 Corinthians to read sequentially Paul's own versions of his insightful moment.

---

[1] Caravaggio's (1571-1610) "Conversion of Saint Paul" captures the full earthy quality of the scene. Those familiar with horses will immediately note that the horse's tail is raised. What might Caravaggio be suggesting?

[2] See Richard Carrier on the possible sources of Acts. While I personally do not necessarily agree with his findings, they merit literary consideration.

The first account that Paul gives of his conversion is found in 1 Corinthians. In this epistle, Paul seems to date his conversion to the very time of the resurrection of Jesus.

> For I delivered to you as of first importance what I also received, that Christ died for our sins in accordance with the scriptures, that he was buried, that he was raised on the third day in accordance with the scriptures, and that he appeared to Cephas, then to the twelve. Then he appeared to more than five hundred brethren at one time, most of whom are still alive, though some have fallen asleep. Then he appeared to James, then to all the apostles. Last of all, as to one untimely born,[1] he appeared also to me. (1 Corinthians 15: 3–8)

Are we to assume from this account that this apparition was the source of Paul's knowledge about Jesus? Surely, if this account has any truth, it nullifies the story in Acts. Of course it might be argued that Jesus appeared to Paul "last of all" does not mean last of all in the immediate sequence of events following the resurrection. It may mean that Jesus appeared to him a very great time later. Yet, from the way the verse reads sequentially this does not seem to be the case.

The Greek for the verse reads "ἔσχατον" (eschaton), which Strong's Concordance translates as "last, at the last, finally." When we look further in Strong's work, he offers extended examples of the word's use. In the expanded list we find the word is used to denote something in an immediate sequence of events of things or people. While it is clearly impossible for us to know exactly what Paul was telling his readers, it would seem that Paul meant Jesus appeared to him immediately after the resurrection, just after he appeared to the other disciples. The curious part of this verse is what Paul does not say. He does not say that there was a time lapse of several years before Paul experienced this visitation. If Jesus appeared to Paul only much later, why would not Paul say, "after I had been in Arabia," or "Some three years later Jesus appeared to me"?[2] If this mystical event occurred just after the resurrection as the last (eschaton) in a series of appearances of the risen Jesus, then there is a clear problem not only with Paul's other epistles such as Galatian but with the events recounted in Acts. In Galatians, Paul notes that he persecuted the first Christians sometime early at the start of the community.

---

[1] "Untimely born" is a most curious description. What does Paul mean by these words? The Greek text reads "ἔκτρωμα" (ektroma), which means something like a miscarriage or an abortion. Indeed, Jerome's Vulgate reads "tamquam abortivo." This is also how it is translated in the French, "comme à l'avorton" and in the Italian, "come a un aborto." The German, however, resembles the English "untimely born," "als einer unzeitigen Geburt." The Jerusalem Bible offers a most interesting if not rather loose translation, "It was as though I was born when no one expected it."

[2] See Galatians 1: 16-19.

> For you have heard of my former life in Judaism, how I persecuted
> the church of God violently and tried to destroy it; and I advanced in
> Judaism beyond many of my own age among my people, so extremely
> zealous was I for the traditions of my fathers. (Galatians 1:13–14)

If Paul received his inspiration from Jesus at the time of the Resurrection, as he claims in First Corinthians, why did he subsequently turn to persecute the followers of Jesus, as Acts would have it, or as he himself says in Galatians? The Galatians account of Paul as an early persecutor of the church would correspond temporally to the conversion tale in Acts, a tale that Paul does not mention. Yet it would seem that this passage in Galatians would be just the right place to round out his story and to demonstrate that, while he persecuted the church, he eventually came to lead it. Instead of the Acts conversion scene, a tale surely too commonplace for Paul's imagination, Paul creates something of a cosmological and metaphysical illumination.

In Galatians, Paul claims that his conversion was no simple event, of his own choosing, made at a moment of adult deliberation. In this epistle Paul claims that his calling was the result of a divine plan beyond and before his very birth.

> But when he who had set me apart before I was born, and had
> called me through his grace, was pleased to reveal his Son to me, in
> order that I might preach him among the Gentiles... (Galatians 1:15)

This is certainly quite a claim. It would seem from this statement that Paul sees himself as something and someone quite remarkable: almost a "fourth" person to be added to the Trinity. Clearly, in his own words, Paul has a most impressive notion of his role in the salvation plan. This "election" was such that it filled Paul with all he needed to know. It empowered him in his entire enterprise. Indeed, Paul asserts most brazenly that because of his special status, conferred by grace, he did not need to confer with any living persons for further information. He already knew on his own all there was to know about Jesus and Jesus' message. So complete was his conviction that he pointedly snubs any visit to Jesus' actual disciples and goes instead to travel abroad for reasons that he does not explain. "I did not confer with flesh and blood, nor did I go up to Jerusalem to those who were apostles before me, but I went away into Arabia; and again I returned to Damascus." (Galatians 1: 16). Only after a time away in Arabia does he return to Syria and Palestine: the distance of time and place seeming to underscore his inspirational independence. For only after this time does Paul finally admit to conferring with Peter and James. Yet, this conference does not seem to influence him, for he then stresses that the visit was only for two weeks.

> Then after three years I went up to Jerusalem to visit Cephas, and
> remained with him fifteen days. But I saw none of the other apostles

except James the Lord's brother. In what I am writing to you, before God, I do not lie! (Galatians 1: 16–20)[1]

When we compare these two epistles we have to ask, was Paul converted at the time of the Resurrection when the gospels say Jesus appeared to many of his followers, or was Paul's change of heart something that took place later because of some pre-determined divine gift prior to his birth, as he claims in Galatians 1?

In 1 Corinthians, Paul claims that he is one "untimely born" who is visited by Jesus. In Galatians, Paul tells his readers that he is "set apart" even before his birth and selected by God's "grace" to preach the Jesus story. These two versions are somewhat perplexing. It would seem that one cannot be both "set apart" before birth and "untimely born" at the same time. So, which is it? Paul does not seem to remember the tales he tells from one letter to the next. This is all the more remarkable, since most scholarship puts the writing of Galatians and 1 Corinthians within the same few years. It is not as though the accounts were written at distant times in his life. We can only surmise that to remember a contrivance is not always as easy as remembering the truth.

As if these two fabrications were not enough, Paul spins yet a third and equally fantastical yarn in 2 Corinthians. In this epistle the divine inspiration that enlightens Paul seems to combine the essential elements found in 1 Corinthians and in Galatians. In 2 Corinthians, Paul not only claims some sort of divine inspiration as he does in Galatians but he sets the event in something of a resurrection scene found in 1 Corinthians. In this way, 2 Corinthians seems something of a hybrid, perhaps a more polished version that he has had time to develop. In this epistle the moment of inspiration becomes a kind of mystical, physical (or metaphysical) experience. In this version, Paul is lifted into the ethers where he partakes of a divine vision.

> I must boast; there is nothing to be gained by it, but I will go on to visions and revelations of the Lord. I know a man in Christ who fourteen years ago was caught up to the third heaven—whether in the body or out of the body I do not know, God knows. And I know that this man was caught up into Paradise—whether in the body or

---

[1] The mention of James recalls the other brother of Jesus, Jude, whose descendants may not have been completely occupied with the same zeal for evangelization. Eusebius in his *Church History* retells a story of them as simple farmers. "Of the family of the Lord there were still living the grandchildren of Jude, who is said to have been the Lord's brother according to the flesh. ... Then they showed their hands, exhibiting the hardness of their bodies and the callousness produced upon their hands by continuous toil as evidence of their own labor. And when they were asked concerning Christ and his kingdom, of what sort it was and where and when it was to appear, they answered that it was not a temporal nor an earthly kingdom, but a heavenly and angelic one, which would appear at the end of the world." Chapter 20.

out of the body I do not know, God knows–and he heard things that cannot be told, which man may not utter. On behalf of this man I will boast, but on my own behalf I will not boast, except of my weaknesses. Though if I wish to boast, I shall not be a fool, for I shall be speaking the truth. But I refrain from it, so that no one may think more of me than he sees in me or hears from me. And to keep me from being too elated by the abundance of revelations, a thorn was given me in the flesh, a messenger of Satan, to harass me, to keep me from being too elated (2 Corinthians 12: 1–7).

By the time Paul had crafted this version, he seems to have found a balance between the bombastic claim of Galatians and the self-deprecation of 1 Corinthians. (Surely, this version is a far cry from the earthy conversion on the road to Damascus as describes in Acts.) Here, while he is still able to "boast," he does not do so from the Paul that we see in front of us, the Paul of mortal flesh. Paul can boast because of "this man": the "other" Paul, who was taken up into heaven. It would also seem that he has learned to keep his "elation" in check by a certain "thorn," a "messenger from Satan." Reading these verses, we begin to wonder if this entire passage is not Paul squirming out of some specific criticism for his self-important pomposity. And who is the "Satan" who wounds him "in the flesh"? Is this a return barb against a then known specific and influential member of Paul's community who was the source of the criticism? This is a most appealing and plausible notion, particularly when one considers the play on words with the Hebrew word "Satan" which literally means "the obstructer" or "the accuser."[1] With the possibility of this passage as a self-justification with a counter attack on his accuser, it takes on a very different meaning. The Greek in which Paul was writing uses the term διάβολος (diabolos). While this term generates the word "devil," that was not at all its original meaning. The Greek "diabolos" meant "slanderer." This seems to be precisely what Paul is saying about whoever it was who wounded him in the flesh.[2]

What reason other than pure fiction, pure invention or outright lying can account for these three different tales? How, if any one of these events actually took place, would the event not be so significant as to be unalterable and unforgettable? But when we consider the discrepancies between these accounts coupled with the bombastic and self-aggrandizing language with which they are delivered, what else can we conclude but that these are the

---

[1]   In Hebrew the word "satan" is most often used with the definite article "The." We would, for example, then read "*the* accuser," and not "Satan." "Satan" is not a personal name. See Crenshaw, James L. *Harper Collins Study Bible* (NRSV), 1989

[2]   It must be noted here for completeness that there are some who read this passage and see in it that Paul had received the "stigmata," the five wounds of Jesus: hands, feet and side. See the medieval legend of Francis of Assisi and the modern accounts of Padre Pio.

puffed up exaggerations of a shameless prevaricator? After all, to remember and recount the truth is usually easy; to recall the details when the story is a lie may be problematic.

Is it so outrageous and irreverent to accuse Paul of dishonesty? Could the self-proclaimed apostle to the Gentiles be a man of little integrity? Again, let us look at Paul's own words. Here is another passage from 2 Corinthians, a passage that is never cited from the pulpit.

> Did I commit a sin in abasing myself so that you might be exalted, because I preached God's gospel without cost to you? I robbed other churches by accepting support from them in order to serve you. And what I do I will continue to do, in order to undermine the claim of those who would like to claim that in their boasted mission they work on the same terms as we do. For such men are false apostles, deceitful workmen, disguising themselves as apostles of Christ. And no wonder, for even Satan disguises himself as an angel of light. So it is not strange if his servants also disguise themselves as servants of righteousness. Their end will correspond to their deeds. (2 Corinthians 11: 12–15).

In other words, Paul is not above taking money from groups not associated with his mainstream followers. Furthermore, he seems to have no qualms about continuing the deceit when it serves his purpose. To defend his position of unethical behavior, Paul argues that he does so for the benefit of his community. Yet, no matter how we look at it, no matter the reason, Paul admittedly practices deceit. If he is willing to rob in order to serve his personal agenda, why would he not equally be at ease with lying about his own conversion in order to do the same thing? Moreover, if he is willing to rob and lie in these situations, what is to prevent him from inventing anything else he may have to say about his very subject, Jesus? After all, one thing all three accounts have in common is that what he tells us about Jesus he did not learn from other men. Why then would his whole concept of Jesus not have been pure fiction?

As noted at the outset of this discussion, Paul's epistles are not the only source of the story of his conversion. For the traditional and far more dramatic version of this tale, we turn to the account in the Acts of the Apostles. Exactly when "Acts" was composed is not certain, but most scholarship generally sets it sometime after Paul's epistle to the Galatians. What may be more certain is that the book of Acts was written before Paul's death, since Acts does not mention that event.[1] Acts presents a version quite different from any of Paul's three contrivances. In Acts, Paul's conversion is

---

[1] Despite fear of entering into nonsensical conjecture, I would also mention that there is a possibility that Paul did not die in Rome as tradition has it. In Paul's Epistle to the Romans, one of his last, he tells of setting off for Spain. (15:24-28). Did Paul end his life there? The place of Paul's death is a subject that merits its own investigation.

not the pre-destined and divine inspiration that Paul speaks of. It is not a highly metaphysical intuition or a visit to a celestial sphere. In Acts, Paul experiences a fully physical and earthly phenomenon.

> Now as he journeyed he approached Damascus, and suddenly a light from heaven flashed about him. And he fell to the ground and heard a voice saying to him, "Saul, Saul, why do you persecute me?" And he said, "Who are you, Lord?" And he said, "I am Jesus, whom you are persecuting; but rise and enter the city, and you will be told what you are to do." (Acts 9:3–6)

Such a striking and miraculous event! Blinded by a bolt of heavenly light, thrown from a horse, cast to the ground and haunted by an unseen voice! Now, why, we must ask ourselves, if a person were to go through such an assuredly physically and psychologically explosive event would he never mention it in his most personal writings: his epistles? Paul never says a word about the road to Damascus in any of his letters. Moreover, not only is Paul silent on this Damascus version, but he contradicts it with the three others versions he narrates in Galatians and 1 and 2 Corinthians. If such an event took place, would Paul, who is otherwise most ebullient, be silent on the subject? With such a history as Acts accounts, why would Paul go to the trouble of inventing not only one, but three other different accounts of his conversion? Clearly, the "Road to Damascus" tale as recounted in Acts is a completely independent fabrication.[1] It is, as is the case with no small number of other in the New Testament tales, a literary invention with only the slightest, if any, historical foundation, created to propound the writer's point of view.

What can we take from these observations of Paul's conversion? There are four distinct accounts; they cannot all be true. But if some are false, how can we think that any of them is true? In the case of Acts, it would seem that the author is guilty of no less than contriving some epic event to heighten the heroic qualities of his protagonist. Now, there is nothing particularly wrong with that as far as literature is concerned. The problem, however, is that most Christians do not look at this text as literature but as fact. When we come to Paul, however, we have an author involved in autobiography. Paul is recounting what he expects us to believe as true events in his life. Yet, clearly, this is not at all the case. He bold-facedly proposes three different, presumptuous and invented tales as true accounts of his own personal experience. If Paul cannot be forthcoming about his own life, how then can he possibly provide a truthful account of a man, who, by his own admission,

---

[1] When it comes to the obvious literary contrivances of the book of Acts, I have to give some thought to the work of Richard Carrier who suggests various classical sources for the book's composition.

he never met? If Paul invents the details of his own life, what is to prevent him from inventing the life of Jesus?

Yet, despite his various equivocations, it is Paul who set the foundation of Christian doctrine. It is Paul who fashioned a Jesus Christ not from history or fact but from the machinations of his own imagination. And Paul spelled out quite indisputably that his knowledge of Jesus does not come from any gospel or from any man.

> For I would have you know, brethren, that the gospel which was preached by me is not man's gospel. For I did not receive it from man, nor was I taught it, but it came through a revelation of Jesus Christ. (Galatians 1: 11–12)

How curious it is that Paul's image of Jesus, based on inspiration rather than investigation, came to override all other portraits of Jesus. It is Paul, far more than the synoptic gospels, that set Jesus up as the sacrifice offered to atone for sin. It is Paul who "preach(es) Christ crucified" (1 Corinthians 23). And it is Paul who declares, "If Christ has not been raised, then our preaching is in vain and your faith is in vain"(1 Corinthians 15:14). Here is the foundation of the notions of sacrificial crucifixion followed by resurrection from the dead, two of the most irrational doctrines of Christianity.

From the outset it is Paul who sets his parameters for a new religion. If the account in Acts has any basis in fact, the early followers of Jesus were devout Jews committed to following Mosaic Law who met for prayer in the temple (Acts 2:46). It is Paul who divorces the followers of Jesus from adherence to the Law of Moses. Nowhere is Paul's overriding influence more clear than in his argument with Peter. Peter, who knew Jesus, saw himself as an observant Jew. For Peter, Jesus' teachings were an extension of Judaism. In Peter's view, those who saw Jesus as a teacher, or even as the Messiah, were still subject to Mosaic Law: particularly the requirement for circumcision. Furthermore, it is worth noting that among these early followers, there was no established concept of the term "Christian." They called themselves followers of The Way (Acts 9:2). (The term "Christian" first appears in Acts 11: 26. "For a whole year they met with the church, and taught a large company of people; and in Antioch the disciples were for the first time called Christians.") In his drive to fashion the religion he envisions, Paul confronts Peter directly and contends that gentiles who turn to Jesus are not obligated by Mosaic Law and were not required to submit to circumcision.

> But when Cephas (Peter) came to Antioch I opposed him to his face, because he stood condemned. For before certain men came from James, he ate with the Gentiles; but when they came he drew back and separated himself, fearing the circumcision party. And with him the rest of the Jews acted insincerely, so that even Barnabas was

carried away by their insincerity. But when I saw that they were not straightforward about the truth of the gospel, I said to Cephas before them all, "If you, though a Jew, live like a Gentile and not like a Jew, how can you compel the Gentiles to live like Jews?" We ourselves, who are Jews by birth and not Gentile sinners, yet who know that a man is not justified by works of the law but through faith in Jesus Christ, even we have believed in Christ Jesus, in order to be justified by faith in Christ, and not by works of the law, because by works of the law shall no one be justified. (Galatians 2:11–16)

Note in this passage the reference to the "circumcision party." Although the original Greek does not use the term "party," the idea is the same. Peter, who was the leader of that group, was found eating with Gentiles and so would be guilty of breaking kosher. Rather than be accused, he withdrew from them. Paul contends that Peter is being hypocritical since while he will break Mosaic Law to eat with non-Jews, he refuses to cede the requirement for circumcision.

For the outcome of the dispute we have to turn to the Acts of the Apostles. There we read that the argument came before the assembly at Jerusalem. In Acts, Peter is given a speech that contradicts his probable position on the obligation of Mosaic Law. In this passage, Peter sounds more like Paul.

God... made no distinction between us and them [gentiles], but cleansed their hearts by faith. Now therefore why do you make trial of God by putting a yoke upon the neck of the disciples which neither our fathers nor we have been able to bear? (Acts 15: 8–10).

As leader of the assembly (and as Jesus' brother) James declares: "....my judgment is that we should not trouble those of the Gentiles who turn to God" (Acts 15:19). It is Paul, then, who has his way. It is Paul who severs the Jesus movement, during his time called "the people of The Way," from its Jewish roots. Furthermore, it is Paul who opens his new religion to the world of the gentiles where he is the primary spokesman.

I have written you quite boldly on some points, as if to remind you of them again, because of the grace God gave me, to be a minister of Messiah Jesus to the Gentiles with the priestly duty of proclaiming the gospel of God, so that the Gentiles might become an offering acceptable to God, sanctified by the Holy Spirit (Romans 15:15).

Paul sets himself up as the apostle to the gentiles. He will present his Jesus to the Roman world. Yet, who is the Jesus that he describes to them? Not only does Paul divorce his new religion from the Judaism where it was born, but he goes on to elaborate an entire theology that will eventually be the cornerstone of his religion: a theology that he says is based personal knowledge of Jesus from divine sources. Paul has not learned what he knows from those followers of Jesus who actually knew him.

In 1 Thessalonians, generally held to be the oldest of Paul's extant epistles, Paul sets out one of his most salient inventions—what among Christian fundamentalists is called the "rapture." Paul begins this notion by establishing that Jesus was killed by the Jews who also now persecute him (1 Thessalonians 2:15). Paul then goes on to affirm that "Jesus died and rose again" and that those "who have fallen asleep in him" (1 Thessalonians 4:14) will also rise. The event will take place with epic proportions: loud cries, archangels and trumpets. "After that," Paul contends, "we who are still alive and are left will be caught up together with them in the clouds to meet the Lord in the air" (1 Thessalonians 4:17). The passage bears a resemblance to Paul's elevation into his third heaven where in one version he received his enlightenment (2 Corinthians 12:55–56). The overall image may also have engendered the prophecy of Matthew's Jesus where we "will see the Son of man coming on the clouds of heaven with power and great glory" (Matthew 24:30). Paul's notion of the second coming is one of the very few passages where Paul's Jesus corresponds with the Jesus of the gospels. The other significant corresponding passage is Paul's account of the institution known as the Eucharist.

> For I received from the Lord what I also delivered to you, that the Lord Jesus on the night when he was betrayed took bread, and when he had given thanks, he broke it, and said, "This is my body which is for you. Do this in remembrance of me." (1 Corinthians 11: 23)

The opening verse of this passage is the most significant. Here Paul reinforces his assertion that what he knows does not come from others but from divine inspiration. In this case, while the inspiration may not necessarily be divine, it would seem that the notion is indeed his. It is Paul who has invented the phenomenon of the Eucharist. That Paul is its creator is all the more evident when we look at what else Paul knows, or does not know, about the Jesus of the gospels. In effect, he knows nothing. Paul makes no mention of a virgin birth. He quotes not a word from the Sermon on the Mount or from the Lord's Prayer. Paul's Jesus is an independent creation.

The one place where Paul's Jesus and the Jesus of the gospels share identical words is in this Eucharist passage. Since Paul's writing pre-dates the gospels, it would seem most probable that the gospels take this notion not from their various lives of Jesus but from the writings of Paul. If Paul is telling the truth when he claims never to have consulted anyone and that he "received" these words "from the Lord" (in other words, invented them), then he is the originator of the Eucharist ritual. If Paul took these words from an already existing practice, then he is once again lying. As we will see later in Chapter 5, the words of Eucharistic institution are not found in the earliest known Christian communion rite.

Of equal importance to Paul's Eucharist invention is Paul's interpretation of the fall of Adam and Eve, a notion that is not at all present in the gospels. In the last of his extant epistles, Paul establishes the doctrine that "sin entered the world through one man, and death through sin, and in this way death came to all men, because all sinned" (Romans 5:12).

Paul does not use the term "Original Sin." That phrase would be developed by a later age, particularly by Saint Augustine.[1] It is, however, Paul who plants the seed of the "Birth Sin" doctrine that went on to shape Christian thought. Here again, this doctrine is an invention of Paul. As already noted, the Jesus of the gospels never even mentions Adam or Eve or the Fall. It is to the question of the Fall that we now turn in Chapter 4.

---

[1] See Chapter 4.

CHAPTER 4. GENESIS: "IN THE BEGINNING"

Any consideration of Christianity's doctrines must begin with the text that serves as the source of all theological development, Genesis. This first book of the bible is the root of the doctrines of sin, redemption, death and resurrection. All of Christian theology and most Christian rituals stem from the theology engendered by this book. Here we find the notion that at some primal time humankind transgressed the will of god and was punished with the curse of mortality. Subsequent to that first offense, all humankind has inherited the guilt of the mythical first ancestors. We are all born with the stain of that first sin upon our souls. The church teaches that it is only the sacrificial blood of Jesus, shed on the cross, that cleanses us from that "Original Sin." It is also through the redemption of Jesus that we will all be restored to life "at the last trumpet" (1 Corinthians 15:52) in the great resurrection.

The Genesis story of the Fall, the sin of Adam and Eve, sets Christian doctrine in motion. Yet, I must ask, how well do most Christians know this story, or rather how well do they know the *two* creation stories in this book? Moreover, even if we know them, we should ask ourselves, have we subjected these tales to the analysis of reason? The creation myth is most curious on two levels. We will look at the story first from a secular point of view and then from a scriptural perspective.

For most educated and sophisticated Christians, I would venture to say that the biblical story of Adam and Eve is taken as a metaphor. Except for those fundamental "creationist" Christians who hold that dinosaurs walked the earth at the same time as humankind, most Christians readily accept Darwin's explanation of evolution and the understanding that the creation story of the bible is little more than a primitive tale.[1] We know, for example, that the earth was not created in seven days. We know that the development of plant and animal species was a gradual and lengthy process that took millennia after millennia. We know that a man did not spring ready-made from the earth or a woman as the by-product of a pilfered rib. Humankind evolved ever so slowly and the time of the modern species is but the smallest fraction of the process. During that gradual development, it can hardly be said that at a given point a specific couple was miraculously endowed with reason and much less that at a given point the couple committed some sin of defiance against their creator. Thus, while today's Christians realize our evolutionary heritage, they cling for some unseen reason to an underlying belief in the notion of some primal fall from grace on the part of our remote and mythical ancestors. If they do not confess belief in it from a scientific view, they believe in it by the practice of Christian doctrine and ritual. I would ask, therefore, if there was no Adam and Eve, how could there have been a fall from grace? If there was no fall from grace how can there be a need for a savior to redeem that fall? Whether the primal offense was committed by some unknown ancestor or by a literal or metaphoric Adam, the Christian system requires that there be some specific individual who is responsible for the sin and another for the redemption. If, however, there were no specific primal parents how can they have transgressed their creator and how can there be a Fall and associated sin? If there is no Fall, the doctrine of Jesus as redeemer simply does not follow logically. With no unique primal parents, there is no Fall; with no Fall there is no sin, and with no sin there is no need for redemption. Thus, while most Christians who consider themselves above blind-eyed fundamentalist literalism might intellectually reject the Adam story, their un-thought-out acceptance of Christian doctrines such as Original Sin and blood redemption affirms it. How this participation in doctrines that defy all reason continues—in a post-Darwin world—defies explanation.

But let me move from further elaboration of this clear affront to reason. In a more studied examination of the Genesis story from a scriptural perspective, we will see that even the bible itself does not support the Christian doctrine of sin and redemption.

Our knowledge of Adam's fall is brought to us in the first book of the bible, Genesis. I would guess, however, that few Christians, even those who can quote chapter and verse, have read Genesis closely. Few readers of the

---

[1] This reference is something of an embarrassment. This mentioned location should not even be acknowledged. Nonetheless I do so because it represents the barring of human reason. How is it possible that there can be so many who flock to Ken Ham's "Creation Museum"? How can willful ignorance support and build an enterprise dedicated to such nonsense as "homology" and the reconstruction of Noah's ark?

text realize that the creation story of Genesis is not a single tale. There are indeed two distinct myths that have been laid out one after the other. The two tales derive from distinctly different sources that were sewn together sometime around the 6th century before the Christian era. While the two tales are generally read as one, the second as an elaboration of the first, the unbiased reader with some patience and attention will see that Genesis very clearly and very distinctly presents two unrelated stories of the creation of the world and its first inhabitants. The first story, the story that is forgotten, is a creation story of goodness and happiness and blessing. The second story, the one that Paul and most Christians ascribe to, is a story of testing and tempting and fall and punishment. The two stories may be divided as follows: the first story runs from Genesis 1: 1 to Genesis 2: 3. The second story runs from Genesis 2: 4 to Genesis 3:24.

How do we know that there are two distinct stories? There are several indicators. Working somewhat in reverse, we look first at the concluding verses of the first story. The narrator tells us,

> And on the seventh day God finished his work which he had done, and he rested on the seventh day from all his work which he had done. So God blessed the seventh day and hallowed it, because on it God rested from all his work which he had done in creation. (Genesis 2:2–3)

It does not take a scholarly analysis to quickly observe that these are the concluding verses of the first story. God has finished his work and he has blessed it. The first tale has ended. We now move to the next verse, Genesis 2:4. This verse is without question the beginning of another story. It is not, as some would have it, an elaboration of the first. Even a cursory reading of the verse immediately indicates that this is the start of another tale. Genesis 2:4 begins, "These are the generations of the heavens and the earth when they were created in the day that the Lord God made the earth and the heavens." Clearly, this verse is the introduction to a second story.

The distinct closing and opening verses, however, are not the only indications of two independent creation accounts. Another indicator is far more emphatic and convincing. In each story, the narrator uses a different set of words for "god." The distinction between the two appellations for "god" has long been recognized by biblical scholars. But one does not have to be a biblical scholar to note the differences. In the first story the creator is called "God," (Hebrew: Elohim); in the second, the creator is identified as "Yahweh God," or "Lord God" (Hebrew: Yahweh Elohim).[1]

The reasons for the distinction between the terms God and Yahweh God are beyond the scope of this study. The history and etymology of the two terms is complex and belong to the realm of biblical scholars. As

---

[1] See, among other translations, *The Hebrew Name Bible*.

I have mentioned before, while every attempt has been made to assure a scholarly approach to this study, high academic research is not our intent. Our purpose here is to offer examples and illustrations based on simple reason and common sense in an appeal to the average reader. Thus, even without a scholarly background to aid in making the distinction between the two terms used for god in Genesis, the average reader can determine the difference rather objectively. Furthermore, there are clear indications that we are dealing with two distinct stories by yet another method. The careful reader can distinguish the two tales by obvious differences in the narrative elements of each.

The first story is one that is told by an agriculturalist. This narrator is clearly aware of plants and how they grow from kindred seed. He knows how the seasons work and that the seasons are in place for plantings and harvests. He has his idea of how the heavens operate and how the land and the seas play their part. This author is more than cognizant of the fundamentals of a civilized society: a society that depends on agriculture for its subsistence. Most important however is that the author of the first creation story envisions a god who is happy with the fullness of his creation and blesses it. This first story is one of hope and promise. It is a story that tells of a civilization that will store grain for future needs, a society that will develop writing to account for their stores and plan for a future. Theirs is a world of blessing.

The author of the second tale, however, seems to have a very different view of humankind. This writer does not seem to be concerned with agriculture or with the stars or with the world beyond his immediate existence. The second author seems perhaps to be a nomadic herder. For this author, life is a hardship. He seeks to understand such things as why humankind must toil, why women have pain in childbirth and even why snakes do not have legs. For this author there was once a paradise, an oasis with plentiful running waters and lush greenery: an oasis that was lost long ago and that has left him little more than an arid wasteland, east of Eden (Genesis 3:24).

The first Genesis story is quite a remarkable account of creation that tells us a great deal about the ancient world's notion of the universe and of life on earth. To begin with, it would seem that creation is not from nothing. The earth (or the land[1]) seems to exist in some kind of unshaped form and there appears to be water that is likewise unformed (1:1–2). The creation of light is most intriguing. In the first story, light is an entity that exists in and of itself. It is not at all associated with the sun or the moon or the stars. Similarly, darkness exists on its own and is, in this story, an element that is separated from light (1: 3–5). The god of the first tale acts on the apparently previously

---

[1]   See the HNV which leaves the Hebrew "eretz" (land).

existing waters, and he divides the waters "above" from the waters "below" and set in place a "*firm*-ament," a divider or heavenly dome of sorts that keeps the waters apart. While the notion of the waters "below" may be apparent, it takes a moment to think in terms of the ancient world to realize that the waters "above" refers to the blue waters of the heavens, the waters that must be the source of rain. The verses that follow surely suggest a narrator who was quite familiar with agriculture. He notes that seed-producing plants were set on the earth that generate according to their kind (1:12). Then lights are set into the dome, "the firmament," that will govern day and night and determine the seasons of the year (1:14). Surely, these elements would be of significance to a society that depended upon a knowledge of the seasons and planting and harvesting times. Finally the god of this tale creates man, a creature he commands to be fruitful and to multiply and to whom he has given dominion over all things including fish, birds and cattle. He then gives his creation all the plants that grow to be his food (1:27–30). In conclusion the god of the first story is happy with his creation and bestows on it his blessing (1:31–2:3). The tale is one of joy and happiness. It tells of a god who has given a world of great abundance to his creation, man. There is no test, no curse, no punishment. The first story is not one of Original Sin. It is a tale of Original Blessing.

As in the first tale, creation in the second story does not take place out of nothing. The earth is already in place but the ground is barren since it had not rained. Then, for a reason that is not given, a mist comes up and god forms man from the clay (2: 4–7). Of interest at this point is that the second story makes no mention of the sun, the moon or the stars. There is no talk of light and dark, no mention of land or sea. What this tale does mention, however, is the essential notion of a garden in which are planted not one but two trees: the tree of life and the tree of the knowledge of good and evil. The garden, we are told, is watered by a confluence of four rivers, and god places man in that garden to tend it (2:15). Clearly, the image of this garden is that of an oasis. Unlike the first story that is told from an agriculturalist's point of view, this tale seems more like the imagined paradise of a nomad wandering the arid lands of the Middle East. Now comes the catch. The god of the second story, after putting these two trees before his creation, tells his man, Adam, that while he may eat of any of the other trees in the garden, he must not eat from the tree of the knowledge of good and evil, saying, "for in the day that you eat of it you shall die" (2:17). This god then seems to have some feeling for the solitude of his new creation and so gives him a few companions, animals (2:20). Not surprisingly, the animals are little comfort to the man and so god creates him a helpmate, woman (2:22). Now follows the intrigue of the tale, the entrance of the serpent into the oasis of this Eden

(3:1). Before all else it must be noted that the beguiler is a serpent (albeit, as we will see shortly, one with legs, perhaps better imagined as a lizard) and not a demon, not a devil and certainly not Satan. Indeed, there is no devil anywhere to be found in the Old Testament. Since the notion that Adam and Eve were tempted by the devil or Satan is completely erroneous, we must make a bit of a side exposition to consider the very notion of a "devil" in scripture and the correct meaning of the word "satan."[1]

In the Old Testament there is no mention of a devil, from the first five books through to Chronicles, where Satan is mentioned only once. Satan as a defined entity does not appear until the book of Job, and even here Satan is not of himself the doer of evil but only a celestial being who challenges god to test the fidelity of Job. Satan, in the sense of an adversary or of a lawyer, stands before the presence of God. He is not the demon of popular imagination who has been cast forever into Hell. Indeed, God gives Satan power over Job in everything but Job's life.

A telling passage about Satan is found in Zechariah, "Then he showed me Joshua the high priest standing before the angel of the Lord, and Satan standing at his right hand to accuse him"(3:1). Here again, Satan is not a demonic being but rather something of a legal prosecutor who stands in the court of God. (The closest anything in the Old Testament comes to a notion of Satan as a fallen angel is an extended passage in Isaiah the opening verses of which I mention here. "How you are fallen from heaven, O Day Star, son of Dawn! How you are cut down to the ground, you who laid the nations low!" (14:12). As most biblical scholars will be quick to note, this passage refers not to a fallen angel (Lucifer) but to an ancient king of Babylon.

In the Old Testament it is God who inflicts hardships on his people and not a devil or a demon. When Pharaoh moves against the Israelites he is not prompted by a demon. Pharaoh is moved by God himself, "And the Lord hardened the heart of Pharaoh, and he hearkened not unto them; as the Lord had spoken unto Moses"(Exodus 9:12). And when Saul is troubled and his advisors suggest someone who can play the harp to sooth him, it is because, "the Spirit of the Lord (Yahweh) departed from Saul, and an evil spirit from the Lord troubled him"(1 Samuel 16:14).

In the Old Testament it is God himself who wears the opposing masks of antagonist and protagonist. Moreover, should one oppose this with the verse from Isaiah 14:12 that is often translated as, "How art thou fallen from heaven, O Lucifer, son of the morning! How art thou cut down to the ground, which didst weaken the nations?" let me quickly disabuse that objection. The name "Lucifer" is Latin in origin and means "light carrier." It appears

---

[1] As noted in the preface such digressions are like a matryoshka where one thing is inside another.

only after Jerome's Latin Vulgate translation appeared in the fourth century. It seems to be at this point that the attributive name[1] becomes a personal name and that it takes on its current connotations. The word does not have these attributes in the original. The Hebrew reads "הֵילֵל" (helel, or heylel), a word that suggests something like "morning light" or "morning star." The Greek Septuagint reads "ἑωσφόρος" (heosoforos), a word derived from "ἑωσ" (heos), "dawn" and "φόρος" (carry). Thus again we have a word which means "dawn carrier" or "dawn bringer." No suggestion of a demon or a devil is found in either of these two original terms. There is simply no demon or devil in the Old Testament to tempt humankind.[2] But let us return to the Genesis narrative.

As we all know, the snake beguiles Eve by telling her that if she will eat of the fruit she will not die but will become like god, knowing good and evil (3:5). Eve not only succumbs to the serpent's charm but she in turn succeeds in tempting Adam (3:6). Of course, from a strictly theological view, the temptation of the couple should be impossible. Since Adam and Eve were innocent, their souls after their creation were not vitiated by sin. If the couple enjoyed innocent souls, those souls would not have been weakened, and since not in a weakened state they would have had no inclinations motivated by greed or pride. They would therefore not be tempted to heed the serpent's promise that they would become like god and know good and evil. They would have no interest in either goal. Of course, such logic in the narrative cannot be expected. The story is, after all, a myth. It is a primitive attempt to explain humankind's sorry state. The story teller of centuries ago cannot be held to theological or literary logic. Still this myth, as illogical as it

---

[1] See Chapter 9 on "attributive" names.

[2] In the New Testament, however, Satan appears in several places. In the synoptics it is Satan who tempts Jesus while he is wandering in the desert. In this situation, Satan is not unlike the Satan of the book of Job, a being who puts Jesus to the test (Matthew 4:10, Mark 1:14). But there is also something of an innovation in the synoptic passages. In Matthew and Luke, Satan does not stand in the court of God as he does in the Old Testament. In these two gospels, Satan has a kingdom of his own (Matthew 12:26, Luke 11:18).

It is only in Luke that we find the most striking and most demonic depiction of Satan as a corrupting influence. Indeed, we would have to ask — isn't this the image of Satan that fundamentalists (and many others who may never have read Genesis carefully) apply to the simple serpent of the Garden, a creature that is nothing more than a lizard who loses his legs and becomes a snake as a punishment for tempting Eve? Luke tells us, "Then Satan entered into Judas called Iscariot, who was of the number of the twelve; he went away and conferred with the chief priests and officers how he might betray him to them" (Luke 22:3-4).

The confusion of the term Satan with the word devil or demon may arise not only from the role this character plays but also from the Greek Septuagint translation of the Hebrew bible where the Hebrew word "שׂטן" (satan) is translated as "διάβολος" (diabolos), "devil."

is, represents the starting point of a complex Christian theology that began with Paul and evolved over the centuries.

After they have succumbed to the serpent's temptation, their sin opens their eyes. Adam and Eve realize their nakedness. They know shame and they cover themselves with leaves. From a metaphoric view, this is a wonderful moment. Here is cognizant humankind individuated from incognizant nature. It is the moment of human self-awareness, including the fateful knowledge of ultimate death. At this point God, fearful that his creations may eat from the tree of life and thus share his immortality, drives them from the garden (Genesis 3:24). But here again is a most curious breach of logic in the narrative. If Adam and Eve in their state before the fall would not know death, why would God be afraid that by eating the fruit of the second tree they would become immortal? There is clearly a flaw in the logic. While such a mistake in the story line is perfectly acceptable when we look at the story as myth that tries to explain why there is death in the world, it can be quite problematic if we try to apply it beyond the poetic. Yet, applying such a tale beyond the poetic—to where a mythical Original Sin becomes the very foundation of a salvation doctrine—is precisely what Christianity, primarily through the instigation of Paul, has done.

As something of an epilogue, the second creation story then concludes with the various curses imposed upon all the players in the drama. The snake (lizard) who has caused the trouble will lose his legs and crawl upon his belly (3:14). The couple will be driven out of Paradise to dwell among thorns and thistles (3:18). Where the man will earn his bread by the sweat of his brow and the woman will have pain in childbirth. Most threatening of all is the malediction that humankind was made from dust and to dust it will return, "In the sweat of your face you shall eat bread till you return to the ground, for out of it you were taken; you are dust, and to dust you shall return" (3:16–19).

This second version of creation is a "that's why" story, a kind of story told generation after generation by tribal myth keepers to explain why things are the way they are. Why does a man cling to his wife? Why does a snake not have legs? Why does a woman have labor pains? Why is the ground covered with weeds and thorns? Why must we work the earth to live? Why must we die? Building a theology on these questions may well have appeased the questioning minds and hearts of our ancestors, but how can it continue to do so even in our own time? Some of these questions, particularly the latter, are the questions that fuel not only the imagination of Paul, as we will see later, but that have troubled many over the centuries.

The influence of Paul's interpretation of the second Genesis story cannot be stressed enough. It is Paul alone who makes use of it to create his theology. There is no mention of the Genesis story anywhere else in the New Testament.

Examine all four gospels. Look as closely as you may. The Jesus of the gospels never mentions the idea of the fall. Jesus never references Genesis and Jesus never pronounces the name of Adam. Indeed, the name of Adam is used only once in any of the four gospels. Only Luke mentions Adam when he creates his genealogy table to establish Jesus' ancestry. Yet, despite the lack of any reference to Adam or his fall and "original sin," the average Christian would probably say that the notion of humankind's fall from grace is one of Jesus' teachings. As with other Christian assumptions such as Jesus' teachings on love (a subject which we will consider in Chapter 7) the idea of the birth sin originates with Paul and the term "Original Sin" does not appear until the fifth century in the writings of Saint Augustine.[1] Thus, here in this second story of Genesis is the irrational foundation of all the Christian doctrinal contrivances that follow to include the notion of redemption by blood sacrifice and the conquest of death through the resurrection of the body. While Paul, the world of his time and many generations thereafter may be forgiven for their lack of knowledge—concerning not only the mysteries of the universe but of the history of the bible's very creation and development—there can be no such excuse in our world today. To close one's eyes to the explicit literary and mythical inventions in the book of Genesis can be called nothing but willful ignorance. In the next chapter we will consider the impossibility of sin, savior and redemption as Paul conceived them.

---

[1] "And lo, there was I received by the scourge of bodily sickness, and I was going down to hell, carrying all the sins which I had committed, both against Thee, and myself, and others, many and grievous, over and above that bond of original sin, whereby we all die in Adam." Augustine, *Confessions*, Book V

Chapter 5. "By Man Came Death": Paul Invents the Fall

In this chapter we will examine how Paul may have developed the idea of the blood sacrifice of Jesus and the redemption of the world from the mythical sin of the second Genesis story. As this chapter will propose, Paul contrived the notion of the need for redemption from an initial misreading of Genesis, a misreading that continues to the present day among many Christians. We also set out the possibility that Paul adopted and adapted notions found in other ancient cults, Hebrew and pagan, that sought to appease a vengeful god though blood sacrifice and through that sacrifice to compensate for human sin.

Before we move on to specific points, I would like to take a moment to restate one of the initial propositions of this book. I have asked why a rational god would demand a blood sacrifice as a redemption, a buying back.[1] There are two fundamental notions to consider about redemption or recompense for wrong-doing. When it comes to the Christian doctrine of redemption, the notion of Jesus as a redeemer, there are two points that bear examination. The first point is based on the most basic sense of human justice, a sense that demands satisfactory monetary or equivalent compensation from the wrong-doer to the person who has been wronged. Such a notion of justice is not without reason: the concept of restitution or compensation is certainly plausible and harms no one. The second point of justice for wrong-doing is one that touches the deepest sensitivities of the human psyche. This more complex point does not necessarily concern itself

---

[1] The word "redemption" comes from the Latin "re-(d)-empto," which means to "buy back" or "to ransom." The Greek ἀπολύτρωσις (apolitrosis) also suggests the idea of a ransom, see *A Word Study of ἀπολύτρωσις in Colossians* 1:14, Joel Jupp, Deerfield, IL October 1, 2008. In both languages the words suggests something economic: a "buy back."

with restitution or compensation. Rather, it concerns itself with some kind of physical punishment to be administered to the wrongdoer. In this situation the offended person seeks not only compensation for whatever thing may have been done against her or him but also demands that the perpetrator be subject to some kind of physical torture or abuse or even death. In this second situation the offended person will only be satisfied by the physical anguish of the offender. That this mindset demanding physical pain and suffering should exist right up to our own time is certainly disturbing and problematic. That one should create a god who exacts the suffering of his own creation is preposterous and irrational. To claim that such a divine being is exacting justice defies all reason. Such a demand is not justice. It is a vile and pointless vengeance exacted to satisfy violence and vicious retaliation.

The notion that the gods must be appeased by a blood sacrifice dates from the earliest moments of humankind that are lost in history. Ascertaining the reasons behind such a practice belongs in the realm of study of anthropologists, and there is no attempt to explain them here. In the recorded history of the ancient world, however, to which we do have access, we know without question that among Hebrew and Gentile alike the practice continued in their respective cultic rites. In Israel animal sacrifice continued until the destruction of the temple in Jerusalem. In Rome, rites involving animal offerings and the reading of their entrails continued until the closing of the pagan temples under Constantine. For centuries prior to the rise of Christianity, the ritual slaughter of animals on temple altars was the central mode of devotion to the gods throughout the Roman world including Israel.[1]

While blood sacrifice in its earliest forms no doubt included human sacrifice, by the time of Paul the cults of Jerusalem or Athens or Rome had long since replaced human sacrifice with the sacrifice of animals.[2] In ancient Rome, the practice of human sacrifice was certainly gone long before the time of the Republic and even before the time of the most ancient kings. In Israel, the substitution of an animal for a human must surely have occurred very early in their tribal social evolution. In the Old Testament, the archetypal tale of Abraham and Isaac, probably recounted first orally and then later put into writing, is a clear justification for the transition from human sacrifice to animal sacrifice.[3] Even though in the social and religious structure of

---

[1] Some ultra-Orthodox Jews in modern Israel still practice the ritualistic slaughter of chickens at Yom Kippur and a small group of less than 1,000 modern Samaritans slaughter a goat at Passover.

[2] The Roman gladiatorial games began as intended human sacrifice. Whether they continued to be seen as such by the time of the Empire is a study for experts in the field.

[3] There are two very interesting exceptions to human sacrifice. Both of them are unclear as to whether the sacrifice took place. In Greek mythology some sources

the ancient world human sacrifice was seen as barbarous, there may have remained some undercurrent of the practice.

Perhaps an excellent example of this undercurrent is the epistle to the Hebrews. Now, it must be immediately noted that most scholars dismiss Paul as the author of this epistle. Nonetheless, even if the words are not Paul's, the sentiment reveals a thought of the times. We read, "Indeed, under the law almost everything is purified with blood, and without the shedding of blood there is no forgiveness of sins"(Hebrews 9:22). Now, the immediate reference here is certainly to the rituals in the temple of Jerusalem. Yet, there is something in the notion of the phrase "without the shedding of blood" that seems to touch on a deeper significance of the practice. Thus, the sacrifice of the animal's body, usually a burnt offering, is not the element that appeases the god. Rather, the blood itself satisfies.

In the writings of Paul, that same notion of human blood sacrifice must have been waiting just under the surface. For Paul, the blood sacrifice returns to its most primitive form, the sacrifice of the blood not of an animal but of a human being, Jesus. For Paul the shedding of the human victim's blood is the only means that can bring salvation to humankind. "It is the blood of the victim that appeases an angry god. Since, therefore, we are now justified by his blood, much more shall we be saved by him from the wrath of God" (Romans 5:9).

In Paul's mind blood was the only means of appeasing the divine. As we will see in this chapter Paul will develop a new theology based on the notion of human blood sacrifice. Paul will read the crucifixion of Jesus as the sacrifice that redeems sins and guarantees victory over death.

Associated with the blood sacrifice is the essential Christian ritual, the Eucharist, that was developed at about this time. Paul's invention of the Eucharist cult transforms the blood sacrifice into a communal liturgy. In Paul's ritual, the drinking of wine and the sharing of bread enjoin all in a commemoration or reenactment[1] of the original sacrifice of the cross.

In one of his earliest epistles Paul sets out his two most significant points: death came to humankind because of Adam's sin, and humankind will conquer death through the resurrection. "For as by a man came death, by a man has come also the resurrection of the dead"(1Corinthians 15:21). Paul

---

tell us that Agamemnon sacrificed his daughter Iphigeneia. In the Old Testament we read the cryptic tale of Jephthah and his daughter (Judges 11-12), a tale not at all unlike that of Iphigeneia.

[1] Roman Catholic "transubstantiation," Lutheran "consubstantiation," or simple Protestant "memorial." The variations of understanding are questions that merit specific attention and cannot be considered here. I will say, however, that most mainstream churches at least make some effort to dignify the celebration. Yet, I must also sadly note that I have seen Fundamentalist shopping mall communion services that actually served Saltines and Welch's grape juice.

reiterates the notion that humankind must suffer death as a result of Adam's sin in the verse that is said to be the first summary of the concept of Original Sin, not by the specific use of the term but by its definition. "Therefore as sin came into the world through one man and death through sin, and so death spread to all men because all men sinned"(Romans 5:12).

Of course, as we have seen in the previous chapter, Paul is reading as a single tale the two very different creation stories in Genesis. In so doing Paul reads the conclusion of the second tale with the greatest emphasis on the Fall and its subsequent punishments. Paul, of course, is reading with the understanding of his time. He would not be aware of how the two tales were edited sometime around the ninth century before Christ so that they appear as one account. Today's reader, however, with contemporary biblical scholarship at hand, cannot be held blameless in the same way. Today's intellectually honest reader cannot fail to see the errors not only in Paul's reading of Genesis but in the notions of sin and redemption that he constructs from it: notions that he made into the foundation of Christian doctrine.

Let us turn now to an even more implausible if not completely impossible doctrine for which Paul sets the groundwork, the notion of the resurrection of the dead. It is in an earlier epistle where Paul sets out to his community the promise of restoration to life from death,

> But God shows his love for us in that while we were yet sinners Christ died for us. Since, therefore, we are now justified by his blood, much more shall we be saved by him from the wrath of God. (Romans 5:8–9)

Paul invents the Christian epic: the dramatic tale of humankind's fall, the curse of death, the blood sacrifice of the hero and the ultimate resurrection to eternal life. Even before we consider how such notions are based on serious misreadings and severe misconceptions, can we not realize that they are above all barbarous and primitive notions contrary to all rational thought and human knowledge? From where did such notions arise but from Paul the earliest of Christian teachers and writers?

Paul's epic of the murdered and resurrected Jesus is of monumental proportions that speaks to an inner dream of humankind. It is from this epic of death and resurrection that Paul creates a complete and most impossible theology founded entirely on myth. Not only do Paul's notions fly in the face of reason and science but, as we shall see in this chapter, Paul's invention has no foundation in either the book of Genesis in the Old Testament or in the synoptic gospels of the New Testament.

As we have seen in Chapter 4, Genesis details not one but two distinct creation stories. The reader will recall that the first Genesis story is clearly a story of joy and happiness. In this story God is pleased with his creation and the story concludes with God's blessing. In the second story, however, we find that God has created two beings who transgress his will. In this second version of the creation myth, humankind is cast from the garden of delights and is charged to work by the sweat of the brow. This second story is unfortunately the one that most people know and upon which Paul has based his unfounded notion of Adam's sin and the Fall.

Why, we might ask, has Paul ignored the first story with an "original blessing" and turned instead to the second story with its "original sin?" When we view his preference for the damnation story over the blessing story in context with the rest of Paul's writings, we may find some evidence for his proclivity. Paul likes to thunder. From his epistles it would seem rather evident that Paul is something of a fire-and-brimstone preacher, a bible thumper who seems to delight in the lightning bolts of his own words. Was there something at the cause of such a temperament? Was there something in Paul's own life that compelled his fiery words and sentiments? We can never know. It would, however, not be difficult to believe that his motivation was based on some earlier personal formation. If there is any truth to Paul's activity against early Christians (as he himself notes and as Acts tells us), we can see that he comes to his new faith already charged with a fiery zealousness.

But let us leave the speculative question of Paul's motivation and continue with the question of the two Genesis stories and how Paul misreads them. The second Genesis story that Paul uses to ground his theology offers no notion that humankind was created to live forever.

Let us look at the notion that our ancestral parents in their innocent state before their transgression would not have known death. This is a notion that is simply not correct, as a careful reading of the text will indicate. If Adam and Eve in their state before the Fall would not have known death, why would God be afraid that they might eat the fruit of the second tree, the Tree of Eternal Life, and thus become immortal? There is clearly a flaw in Paul's perception of this situation, and in the reading of most Christians to this day. While such a mistake in the story line is perfectly acceptable when we look at the story as a myth that tries to explain why there is death in the world, it can be quite problematic if we try to apply it beyond the poetic.

Yet, this is precisely what Christian doctrine has done in those doctrines that emerge from the teachings of Paul. Adam and Eve, in the primal tale, were not free from death. They were intended to die just like any other creature, Fall or no Fall. As you will recall, there are two trees in the second story. The first tree is that of knowledge and the second tree is the tree of eternal life. "And the Lord God said, 'Behold, the man is become as one of us, to know good and evil: and now, lest he put forth his hand, and take also of the tree of life, and eat, and live forever' "(Genesis 3:22). If we follow the intrinsic logic of the second story, the fact that eating from the tree of life would have made man eternal, says in so many words that man, even prior to Adam's Fall, was a creature destined to die. If man were to live forever, there would have been no "tree of eternal life" and no prohibition of eating from it. God would not have banished Adam and Eve from Eden in order to prevent them from eating the fruit of eternal life. Adam and Eve were expected to die. There was no time when they did not know death. Paul has clearly misread Genesis. More to the point, today's Christians follow him blindly along.

Paul, in his understanding of the text as he sets it out in Romans 5: 2, has clearly misread the story. There is nothing in Genesis that states or even suggests that humankind in the original creation was a creature who would live forever. A careful and not wishful reading of Genesis is quite clear. Humankind, even in the Genesis myth, was destined to die. If they were not to die, why did the god of this tale forbid them the fruit of eternal life? Paul's statement that "through man came death" has no biblical or literary or rational foundation.

Even when viewed from the more liberal and enlightened notion that the Adam story is metaphor, the essence of the story in Paul's terms suggests that at some point in archaic history humankind, as represented by our primal parents, did not know (experience) death. Such a notion is clearly impossible. All living things by virtue of being living things come to the end of their cycle. They die. Life and death are part of the ongoing cycle of all creation. There was never a time, literally or metaphorically, when any entity was not subject to the finality of its term.

There was no time when humankind did not experience death. Paul's premise and the theology upon which it is based, even to our day, is little more than imaginative and wishful invention. Humankind was never free from death any more than any other living creature from the simple single cell to the great whales of the sea. Is there any living entity from the most simple to the most complex that does not know the moment of finality, the moment that is death? Today's Christians need to raise their consciousness and look at Christian doctrine rationally.

The introduction of the idea that death happens because of the sin of our mythical parents is not the only impossibility that Paul contrives. Paul needs the story of the Fall as a basis for the rest of his invented redemption theology. Paul's vision of 'Jesus the redeemer' can only make sense if there is something to redeem.

Chapter 6. "By His Blood": Jesus as Redeemer

As we have seen, Paul's theological foundation is grounded on his misreading of Genesis. There is clearly nothing in Genesis that supports his teaching. More than that, the second Genesis tale of the Fall is little more than a construct akin to any number of ancient tales. Genesis is in the mythic tradition that attempts to explain why the human condition is "solitary, poor, nasty, brutish, and short."[1] Having suggested Paul's groundless foundation of humankind's misery in his skewed reading of the Old Testament, we now move to the gospels of the New Testament and their view of the role of Jesus.

Paul's epistles predate the gospels. The gospels therefore would not have influenced Paul. Remember too that Paul claims that what he 'knows' does not come the recollections of those that knew Jesus. What Paul knows he claims to have learned from divine inspiration (Galatians 1:16). Now, while the gospels did not influence Paul, it is most probable that the notions of Paul influenced, at least to some degree, the perspective of the writers of the gospels. Paul's possible influence on the gospels is most apparent (particularly in John) when it comes to the teachings of Jesus on love. This is not the case, however, when it comes to Paul's notion of Jesus as a redemptive sacrifice. In the synoptics one would be hard pressed to find any clear and direct mention that Jesus is to be seen as a redemptive blood sacrifice. Indeed, there are only two verses, almost identical in Mark and Matthew, where the idea is mentioned: "For the Son of man also came not to be served but to serve, and to give his life as a ransom for many"(Mark 10:45, Matthew 20:28). Other than these two verses, the synoptic Jesus is silent on the subject. In John's gospel, however, the notion of Jesus as a blood sacrifice

---

[1] *Leviathan*, Chapter XIII, The Incommodities of War, Thomas Hobbes, 1651

is most distinct. It is not, however, proposed directly. It is always presented veiled in metaphor.

Let us begin with the synoptic gospels. When we do a close and unprejudiced reading of the synoptic gospels, we will find little mention of Jesus as a blood sacrifice and no mention whatsoever of a sin to which all humankind is heir. The Jesus of the gospels, including the gospel of John, never mentions the idea of man's fall. Jesus never references Genesis. Jesus never pronounces the name of Adam. Indeed, the name of Adam is used only once in any of the four gospels. It is found only in Luke, where he creates his genealogy table to establish Jesus' ancestry. Yet, despite the lack of any reference to Adam or his fall, much less any mention of an "original sin," the average Christian would probably say that the myth of the Fall and our redemption by Jesus is one of Jesus' teachings. As with other Christian assumptions on the New Testament's pronouncements,[1] the idea of the birth sin or Original Sin is not found in any of the gospels. The general concept of an Original Sin that must be redeemed is found only in Paul. Yet, even Paul never uses those specific terms.

If the idea of the inherited sin of Adam and Eve did not originate with Paul, it may have evolved gradually immediately after the execution of Jesus. It may very well have been that in the earliest years of the Christian cult the notion arose that the Roman's execution of the miracle worker and itinerant preacher, one Jesus of Nazareth, was nothing less than the culmination of a divine plan. One of the very few passages that states that Jesus will save his people is found in the earliest gospel, that of Matthew. In the opening chapter of his gospel at the moment of the incarnation the angel proclaims to Mary, "You shall call his name Jesus, for he will save his people from their sins" (Matthew 1:21).[2] Yet, this passage makes no mention of how that will be accomplished. Will Jesus accomplish the saving of his people through his teachings? Will he become the ruling Messiah of Israel and save his people from Roman rule as we shall in Chapter 8? Or, as Paul sees it, by becoming a human blood sacrifice? The gospel writer does not say. Perhaps the reason was not particularly clear at the time of the writing?

Other passages in the synoptic gospels that refer to the death of Jesus and the purpose of his death are few and unclear. More important, any passage in

---

[1] There is no talk of sexuality. There is no consecration of a priesthood. Despite Roman and Eastern Catholic and certain Anglican beliefs, Jesus never ordained anyone nor ever mentioned anything about a priestly order. In terms of sexuality, and this is a point that Fundamentalists may wish to take note of, Jesus never says a word on the subject.

[2] Compare this announcement with that of the angel in Luke where there is no mention of salvation. Luke's angel predicts Jesus as the heir of David and future king.

the gospels where Jesus speaks of his impending death was clearly added by the gospel authors "after the fact." In the oldest gospel, that of Mark, we read,

> And he began to teach them that the Son of man must suffer many things, and be rejected by the elders and the chief. From that time Jesus began to show his disciples that he must go to Jerusalem and suffer many things from the elders and chief priests and scribes, and be killed, and on the third day be raised. (8:31)

In Matthew we read, "From that time Jesus began to show his disciples that he must go to Jerusalem and suffer many things from the elders and chief priests and scribes, and be killed, and on the third day be raised" (16:21). And again, in Luke, as we might expect of the synoptic, an almost identical verse, "The Son of man must suffer many things, and be rejected by the elders and chief priests and scribes, and be killed, and on the third day be raised" (9:22)..

While Jesus may predict his death, the few passages where he does can be nothing other than later attempts to find some reason for the execution of Jesus at the hands of the authorities.[1] Of course the reader may readily raise the objection that it is only my claim that such predictions were put into the mouth of Jesus after the fact. Certainly, the reader may be correct.[2] But even when looking at those passages where the gospel authors have Jesus predicting his own death, none of them is particularly clear as to why his blood must be shed. Indeed, as we shall discuss in Chapter 8, when Jesus predicts his death in the synoptic, it may be because he sees himself as the messiah king who will die and then be transported to heaven. In this heaven, a real and physical place situated above the "firmament," Jesus will undergo some kind of undescribed metamorphosis. None of the gospels mentions how this may happen. Nonetheless, Matthew and Mark give us a Jesus who foretells the results of that mystical transformation. We read: "Jesus said to him [the high priest at his trial] 'You have said so. But I tell you, hereafter you will see the Son of man seated at the right hand of Power, and coming on the clouds of heaven' " (Matthew 26:64).[3] In Mark we read,

---

[1] He may well have been executed based on other grounds, as we will discuss later in Chapter 8.

[2] See: Funk, Robert W. et al. *The Five Gospels: The Search for the Authentic Words of Jesus*, Harper, San Francisco, 1993. I make no claim for the validity of this text or for the methods used by the Jesus Seminar in arriving at their conclusions. The text is offered only as an example of references to statements that Jesus may not have made.

For my part, critics will be quick to point out that when we come across a passage where Jesus predicts his death, I am quick to determine that this prediction was a later addition. Such critics may be correct, but I would ask them to look at each gospel as a literary whole. If you do so, do you see any of the gospels presenting the death–redemption holistically as a recurrent theme?

[3] See also Matthew 24:30: "Then will appear the sign of the Son of man in heaven, and then all the tribes of the earth will mourn, and they will see the Son of man coming on the clouds of heaven with power and great glory."

"And Jesus said, 'I am; and you will see the Son of man seated at the right hand of Power, and coming with the clouds of heaven'" (14:62).

These verses are again words that the gospel writers put into the mouth of Jesus. The gospel writers, like the earliest Christians, were waiting for an immediate return of Jesus in their own lifetime. Of course, it did not happen then, and it is not happening now.[1]

Furthermore, note that in this passage there is no mention of Adam or humankind's collective fall from grace, but not only that—there is no suggestion that the death of Jesus is intended to redeem innate human sinfulness. What is most curious in both passages is that the author has Jesus conclude with the affirmation that he will rise. If the Jesus of this gospel knew that he would rise, knew that he would overcome death, then what, in keeping with the notion of a perfect sacrifice, would be the value of his bloody death? Is the merit of his death simply that he would suffer horrible agony and that his suffering would appease a blood thirsty and sadistic god? What sense can such a violent death possibly make? If Jesus knew that his death would be overcome by a restoration to life in the resurrection, then his death in itself means nothing. Indeed, his violent death on the cross becomes little more than a sadistic expression designed to appeal to the lowest of human inclinations and interests in all that is the most violent, ambiguously sadomasochistic and humanly destructive.[2]

Even when we move from the synoptic gospels to the metaphysical gospel of John, the notion that the death of Jesus was a blood sacrifice for the inherited sin of Adam is not clearly established. John's gospel, the last to be written, and written well after the time of Jesus, is less a narrative than it is a philosophical declamation wherein Jesus offers long monologues about who he is. In John, Jesus' death prediction becomes a very verbose and abstracted scene. John's Jesus proclaims, "'When I am lifted up from the earth, I will draw all men to myself.' He said this to show by what death he was to die" (John 12:32). Despite what the evangelist tells us, this declaration

---

[1] The never-happening return of Jesus causes much chagrin to no small number of fundamentalist preachers who convince their gullible followers to reject all possessions in expectation of the second coming. My favorite example is that of the radio preacher Brother Harold Camping, who claimed that the "rapture" was scheduled for May 21, 2011, with the final cataclysm on October 21, 2011. I once heard a radio call-in visitor proposed to him that, since Brother Camping was so certain of this catastrophic date, he should sign a paper to turn over the radio station to the caller on the morning following the rapture since, of course, after that, the station would have no purpose. Brother Camping had no response. It would seem that the loss of the millions of dollars he collected from his faithful followers was a bit more significant than the second coming.

[2] Even the literary and pictorial representations of Jesus dying on the cross are shaded with sexual, if not even pornographic undertones: expressions that appeal to the lowest and yet most compelling of human inclinations. What is the underlying message of all those nude images of Jesus on the cross?

says nothing about "*what* death he was to die." Furthermore, there is still no explanation as to the reason for his death.

Of course, the literal critic will be quick to cite John 3:16, "For God so loved the world that he gave his only Son, that whoever believes in him should not perish but have eternal life." But read it carefully, without the previously conceived notions that centuries of Christian doctrine have merged into this verse. Look at the words of the text alone. The verse says that god "gave his son," for us "to believe in him." There is no word about death, or that salvation comes through his death. Rather, it would seem from this verse that salvation comes not from a sacrificial death but from belief in the life and *teachings* of "his son." John's text, despite the possible influence of Paul's notion of the blood sacrifice, looks instead to a Jesus who saves humankind by offering the perfect example of how humankind should live. (See note 24.)[1]

While there is no individual statement from John's Jesus that his death will be the means of redemption, there is a general tone, always expressed metaphorically, indicating that Jesus is the sacrificial lamb. John's gospel sets up the image of Jesus as a blood sacrifice in his portrayal of the baptism of Jesus by the Baptist. In John's gospel alone, the Baptist announces, "Behold the lamb of God who takes away the sins of the world"(John 1:29). While here again there is no mention of *how* he will take away the sins of the world, we can assume that it will be by his death during the Passover. As I have noted earlier, the author of John goes so far as to change the very day of the crucifixion. In John, Jesus dies on the day of preparation for the Passover: the day on which the lambs were slain for the meal.[2] In John, then, Jesus becomes the sacrificial Pascal lamb. Still, it must be recalled that John's gospel is composed well after Paul's theology has had the opportunity to influence the early Christian community, particularly in ritual.

Yet, even with the extended metaphor of the lamb, John's Jesus proposes another reason for his coming into the world. During the passion, John's Jesus testifies before Pilate. "Pilate said to him, "So you are a king?" Jesus answered, "You say that I am a king. For this I was born, and for this I have come into the world, to bear witness to the truth. Everyone who is of the truth hears

[1] This reading is further born out when we consider the epistle of John (although not necessarily written by the same John as the gospel). "And this is the testimony that God gave us eternal life, and that this life is in his Son" (1 John 5:11).

[2] The animal was slain on the eve of the Passover, on the afternoon of the 14th of Nisan, after the Tamid sacrifice had been killed, *i.e.*, at three o'clock, or, in case the eve of the Passover fell on Friday, at two. The killing took place in the court of the Temple and might be performed by a layman, although the blood had to be caught by a priest, and rows of priests with gold or silver cups in their hands stood in line from the Temple court to the altar, where the blood was sprinkled. *Jewish Encyclopedia*, 1906

my voice"(John 18:37–38). The Jesus of John does not at all suggest that he has been sent as a sacrifice.

Here again Jesus informs Pilate that he has been sent to "bear witness to the truth." His purpose is to testify by his teachings and actions. There is, however, in John a passage that is most perplexing not only for today's hopefully rational Christian but for the Jews of the time. Is the author of John not clear himself as to why Jesus came into the world? Why would he set the scene to pose this question and solicit this answer? What became of the image of the sacrificial lamb? John's gospel, for all its philosophical language and metaphysical imagery, can often be quite ambiguous. One of the oddest passages about the flesh and blood of Jesus is found in none other than the gospel of John.

> "I am the living bread which came down from heaven; if any one eats of this bread, he will live forever; and the bread which I shall give for the life of the world is my flesh." The Jews then disputed among themselves, saying, "How can this man give us his flesh to eat?" So Jesus said to them, "Truly, truly, I say to you, unless you eat the flesh of the Son of man and drink his blood, you have no life in you; he who eats my flesh and drinks my blood has eternal life, and I will raise him up at the last day. For my flesh is food indeed, and my blood is drink indeed. He who eats my flesh and drinks my blood abides in me, and I in him." (John 6: 51–56) .

It is somewhat more than difficult to look at this passage immediately and with quick answers.

In the first place, this is the Jesus of John. This is the Jesus of high-minded philosophical notions and of metaphor. This Jesus has nothing to do with the simple itinerant preacher that we find in Mark or any of the other synoptics. This is a Jesus who is speaking with notions that have clearly been developed later in the post-crucifixion Christian community. They are certainly notions dependent on Paul's bread and wine, blood sacrifice ritual. This passage in John also rebukes the Jews, who are the decided evildoers in John's anti-Semitic gospel.[1] Yet these Jews show at least a modicum of reason in their response to what John's Jesus has to say. In the first place, to eat the blood of an animal, much less that of a human, violates the fundamentals rules of kashrut, Kosher. Beyond the legal rules, it is also eminently apparent that what John's Jesus is proposing is offensive to custom and to reason. I would invite anyone to read this passage from John with even a modicum of common sense. It is not only irrational, it is offensive. Even a symbolic

---

[1] The question of John's anti-Semitism is not the concern of this study. John's disapproval of the Jews is somewhat well known. The interested reader would do well to examine the question in detail.

participation in such a primal and barbaric sharing of human flesh and blood is without question nothing less than repulsive to any rational mind.

Yet, even though the narrator of John has taken pains to alter the day of the death of Jesus such that he becomes the sacrificial lamb, I would venture to say that this variation is not apparent to the vast majority of Christians. In fact, no small amount of John's unique depiction of Jesus as the paschal sacrifice has colored the synoptics with tones that they do not contain.

But even when, with reluctance, we set aside the sole arbiter of our knowledge, human reason, the rationale of the Christian held doctrine of a blood sacrifice cannot be logically addressed. Even considering such passages as found in John, nothing clearly determines the bloody crucifixion of Jesus as the means to humankind's salvation.

What makes the absence of any such statement that Jesus' death is the instrument of salvation all the more curious is the realization that each of the four authors was reading back in their narratives and supplying Jesus with a prophecy of his own death that Jesus himself doubtfully ever pronounced. So, why, if the gospel authors take the trouble to provide Jesus with the prophecy of his death, do they not exploit that same moment to allow each of their Jesus' to expound on the reason for his death? Indeed, not only do the gospels fail to substantiate that the crucifixion was the means to atone for sin, the gospels do not even bother to mention anything about the supposed sin itself. Jesus never mentions anything about what will later be called Original Sin, and nowhere does Jesus say anything about the Fall or about Adam. It seems that the Jesus of the gospels is not at all familiar with the sin and redemption theology invented sometime later by Paul.

Having noted that there is no clear indication in the gospels that the crucifixion of Jesus is intended to redeem humankind from sin, I must point out one possible exception. But, here again, the exception is without question influenced by the later inventions of Paul. Of all the sequences in the synoptics that deal with the death of Jesus, there is only one sequence common to all three that suggests that the blood of Jesus is to be shed for the redemption of humankind. The passage is that moment in the synoptics where Jesus shares the bread and wine at his Last Supper as his body and blood. Yet even here, it is only in Matthew that the blood of Jesus is shed for the redemption of sin. (It is also worth noting that the Last Supper "bread-and-wine" sequence is not found at all in John's gospel. Elsewhere, however, John gives his Jesus a most curious description of body and blood expressed metaphorically. The verse somewhat resembles that of Jesus as the water of life in the "woman at the well" sequence. "I am the living bread which came down from heaven; if any one eats of this bread, he will live forever; and the bread which I shall give for the life of the world is my flesh." See John 6: 25–66 as cited earlier for the full speech.)

Take a moment to compare the three versions of this scene as found in the synoptics. In Mark we read: "And he took a cup and he said to them, 'This is my blood of the covenant, which is poured out for many.' And when he had given thanks he gave it to them, and they all drank of it" (14:23–24). In Matthew, the sequence reads, "And he took a cup, and when he had given thanks he gave it to them, saying, 'Drink of it, all of you; for this is my blood of the covenant, which is poured out for many for the forgiveness of sins' "(26: 27–28). And finally in Luke: "And likewise the cup after supper, saying, 'This cup which is poured out for you is the new covenant in my blood' " (22:20).

When we compare these three passages, it is evident that only Matthew clearly states that the blood of Jesus is shed for the forgiveness of sin. It is by comparing these verses that we also see how the point of view of each author determines the words of the text. Just as Matthew is the only author who has his Jesus give a reason for his blood shedding, it is likewise only Matthew who provides some notion of the death redemption in his narration of the incarnation. And Matthew, as the reader may recall from Chapter 2 and as we will elaborate further in Chapter 8, is the only gospel writer who tells us that the name "Jesus" means "savior." So, while Matthew is the only gospel author who seems to have a more fully developed reason for the blood death of Jesus, it is also Matthew whose view that Jesus was a savior who shed his blood not only colors all other gospels but permeates them with a perspective that they do not contain.

The effect of the Last Supper sequence and its notion of the blood of Jesus as a sacrifice poured out for the redemption of sin is essential to Christian doctrine. But it is hardly likely that Jesus ever pronounced the words in any of the three synoptic versions of this sequence. As I have proposed in Chapter 3, the Last Supper ritual formula probably did not originate with the gospels but was created by Paul.

There is a very clear indication that the words of Jesus in this passage are not from Jesus but from Paul. This verse is the only time that Paul professes to quote anything that Jesus had to say. If Paul never cites anything that the gospels purport that Jesus said, why does he quote this Last Supper passage? And since Paul never knew Jesus, and if he is right in saying that all he knows he received as inspiration, it must follow that the Eucharistic words are Paul's own invention. Thus, the synoptics are taking the Eucharistic words from Paul.

Indeed, Paul begins the passage with his standard notice of some kind of personal revelation. In this passage Paul begins by noting, as he has noted elsewhere, that what he knows about Jesus he has received directly "from the Lord" and that he consulted with no one when it came to the teachings of Jesus.[1] In other words, these are words of Paul's own imagination: words and ritual that he invented.

> For I received from the Lord what I also delivered to you, that the Lord Jesus on the night when he was betrayed took bread, and when he had given thanks, he broke it, and said, "This is my body which is for you. Do this in remembrance of me." In the same way also the cup, after supper, saying, "This cup is the new covenant in my blood. Do this, as often as you drink it, in remembrance of me." For as often as you eat this bread and drink the cup, you proclaim the Lord's death until he comes. (1 Corinthians 23–26)

While other early documents indicate that the primitive Christian community gathered together to share some kind of communal meal, they do not mention the bread and wine as sacrificial body elements. The Christian gathering is mentioned in Acts 20:7: "On the first day of the week, when, we were gathered together to break bread, Paul talked with them, intending to depart on the morrow; and he prolonged his speech until midnight." In this passage, written about Paul but not by Paul, there is no mention of the bread breaking as a kind of sacrificial ritual. Nor is there any mention of wine. Furthermore, in another early document, the Didache, which dates from no later than the early second century AD and perhaps as early as the first, the communal meal has nothing to do with a blood sacrifice. It appears to be nothing more than a common sharing of bread and wine. The Didache text, which offers a most detailed instruction on how to celebrate the communal meal, the "Eucharist," does not include the Pauline notion of reenacting a blood sacrifice. We read:

> Now concerning the Eucharist, give thanks this way. First, concerning the cup: We thank thee, our Father, for the holy vine of David Thy servant, which You madest known to us through Jesus Thy Servant; to Thee be the glory forever. And concerning the broken bread: We thank Thee, our Father, for the life and knowledge which You madest known to us through Jesus Thy Servant; to Thee be the glory forever. Even as this broken bread was scattered over the hills, and was gathered together and became one, so let Thy Church be gathered together from the ends of the earth into Thy kingdom; for Thine is the glory and the power through Jesus Christ forever... But let no one eat or drink of your Eucharist, unless they have been baptized into the name of the Lord; for concerning this also the Lord has said, "Give not that which is holy to the dogs."[2] *Chapter 9. The Eucharist.*

---

[1] Acts 20:24, 1 Cr.15:3,

[2] Roberts-Donaldson translation. For other translations see: http://www.earlychristianwritings.com/didache.html

In this passage we read nothing that mentions the death or resurrection of Jesus. There is distinctly no mention that the death of Jesus was a sacrifice for sin or that the bread and wine are references to his body and blood. Furthermore, there is no mention that the Eucharist has anything to do with the redemption of sin. In the Didache the ritual seems to be nothing more than a communal experience, a thanksgiving, a "Eucharist" in the denotative meaning of the word.[1] [2]

In addition to Paul's Last Supper blood-cup invention, there are two other peculiar references to the blood sacrifice of Jesus that hint at some cultic practice. In these two cases, the blood component of the ritual is that of a purifying agent. In each of these references the blood is sprinkled on the participants. And we must ask what this "sprinkling" was. What I propose here may be entirely suppositional. Nonetheless, there is something in the tone of these verses that suggests some kind of early rite: a rite where the adherents may have been sprinkled with real or symbolic blood. The two references are in 1 Peter and in Hebrews. In 1 Peter we read,

> Peter, an apostle of Jesus Christ, To the exiles of the Dispersion in Pontus, Galatia, Cappadocia, Asia, and Bithynia, chosen and destined by God the Father and sanctified by the Spirit for obedience to Jesus Christ and for sprinkling with his blood: May grace and peace be multiplied to you (1:1–2).

In the Hebrew Names Bible, we read a translation of this passage that is highly suggestive that the sprinkling is some kind of ritual. The passage reads: "that you may obey Yeshua the Messiah and be sprinkled in his blood: Grace to you and shalom be multiplied."

The New Jerusalem Bible, a translation considered by many to be the most accurate, we read a similar translation, "...and sprinkled with his blood." In Hebrews we read,

> But you have come to Mount Zion and to the city of the living God, the heavenly Jerusalem, and to innumerable angels in festal gathering, and to the assembly of the first-born who are enrolled in heaven, and to a judge who is God of all, and to the spirits of just men made perfect, and to Jesus, the mediator of a new covenant, and to the sprinkled blood that speaks more graciously than the blood of Abel. (12:22–24)

There is something very "present tense" in the Hebrews passage. When considering the opening words with those of the final verse, the writer seems to be saying "You have come to ...*the sprinkled blood.*" The words seem to be reminders of what these new followers had committed themselves to

---

[1] Greek *eucharisteo = to be thankful.*
[2] The early Christian ritual may very have been a communal dinner not unlike that of the Sikh "langar," still practiced today, where all eat side by side regardless of rank.

through some kind of initiation rite that included some kind of symbolic or actual blood sprinkling.

The notion that the epistle author may be referring to some kind of ritual is all the more evident in the King James version which translates the Greek as, "But Ye are come ... to Jesus the mediator of the new covenant, and *to the blood of sprinkling*, that speaketh better things than that of Abel." When we read the Hebrew Names Bible translation, it seems to suggest the same idea, "to Yeshua [Jesus], the mediator of a new covenant, *and to the blood of sprinkling* that speaks better than that of Hevel [Abel]."

Of course, the notion that some early Christians practiced a blood sprinkling ritual is purely conjectural, but it does not seem totally improbable. When we consult Strong's Concordance[1] for this term, we find that in every case the term "sprinkling" has to do with a purification ritual. Four out of five of uses of the term in the New Testament are found in none other than Hebrews, a very blood-oriented epistle.[2] The Hebrews verses are 9:13, 19, 27 and 10:22; the fifth reference to ritual sprinkling is found in Mark 7:4. The Old Testament reference is found in Numbers 19. Here again "sprinkling" has to do with ritual cleansing.

Of course what I present here is highly speculative. There is nothing that states outright that these passages describe a specific blood ritual. Nonetheless, they are worth considering when looking at the Christian blood sacrifice doctrine. To have these references in mind may also offer some insight into early claims that Christians were not imitating other rituals of the time.

Looking at references beyond the New Testament, one very often finds references which claim that Paul and perhaps other early Christians were imitating the rites of the cult of Mithras, a competitor to early Christianity. While the thought is tempting that the Mithric cult influenced Paul and some of his Christian colleagues, there is really simply no proof that this was the case. Such speculation may often be the province of sensational works on early Christianity.[3] Most important, there are simply no extant copies of Mithric rituals to substantiate the claim. No one really knows the exact nature of their practices. There are only hints from various sculptures, wall paintings and ruins of their sanctuaries. The only mention of Mithric ritual comes from an early Christian writer, Justin Martyr, writing in the second century. Justin, however, looks at it from the opposite perspective. He claims

---

[1] James Strong, 1822–1894, created an index of biblical terms that allows for etymological reference.
[2] In the RSV, the word "blood" is found no less than twenty times in this epistle.
[3] In my high school years, I read H.G. Wells *Outline of History* where he contends that Paul invented Christianity in imitation of Mithric ritual. When I brought this up in religion class, my Augustinian teacher was so outraged that he demanded to see my parents and that they surrender the book. I still have it.

that Christianity has not imitated the Mithras cult but that the followers of Mithras have created a corrupted version of the Christian ritual.

> For the apostles, in the memoirs composed by them, which are called Gospels, have thus delivered unto us what was enjoined upon them; that Jesus took bread, and when He had given thanks, said, "This do ye in remembrance of Me, this is My body "and that, after the same manner, having taken the cup and given thanks, He said, "This is My blood"; and gave it to them alone. Which the wicked devils have imitated in the mysteries of Mithras, commanding the same thing to be done. For, that bread and a cup of water are placed with certain incantations in the mystic rites of one who is being initiated; you either know or can learn. (The First Apology, Chapter LXVI. –*Of the Eucharist.* Cyril C, Richardson translation.)[1]

Having given the benefit of the doubt to Justin, we might just as easily turn his argument around and wonder if the very reason that Justin is making this defense is precisely because the Christians did indeed take the practice from the followers of Mithras and not the other way around. Since, as we have just seen, the Didache makes no mention of blood sacrifice and suggests only some kind of communal sharing of bread and wine, it may very well be that Christians embellished their meal by incorporating aspects of the Mithras blood ritual. One way or another, it makes little difference. The point is that the Eucharist as now practiced with its flesh and blood ritual, whether actual or symbolic, has become a foundational Christian doctrine. The notion of a blood sacrifice, regardless of its origin, is barbaric, primitive and contradictory to any rational mind, and this doctrine flies in the face of all reason.

Still, the doctrine of a blood sacrifice to expiate an imaginary mythical sin has further implications. From his doctrine of sin and redemption, Paul elaborates the subsequent notion of the resurrection of Jesus and the promised resurrection of all humankind. In his first letter to the Corinthians, Paul declares, "The last enemy to be destroyed is death" (15:26).

Paul's theology of freedom from death through the resurrection flies in the face of the simplest common sense and defies all we know of the world we live in. There was never a time when any living creature on earth did not know death. To posit that death is a punishment is absurd. Death is the ultimate destination of all living things. Man and beast, plant and fungus all

---

[1] It is also important to note a reference to the word "sacrifice" in the same text. There is, however, no clarification on its meaning. "But every Lord's Day gather yourselves together, and break bread, and give thanksgiving after having confessed your transgressions, that your sacrifice may be pure. But let no one who is at odds with his fellow come together with you, until they be reconciled, that your sacrifice may not be profaned. For this is that which was spoken by the Lord: "In every place and time offer to me a pure sacrifice; for I am a great King, says the Lord, and my name is wonderful among the nations."

meet an end. Even stone may be said to end up crumbled to dust or turned to ash in a volcano. A resurrection of the dead is simply pointless. Why would a rational god create, then destroy, only to recreate? We will consider the notions of resurrection and ascension in the following chapter.

To conclude this chapter I must again ask the reader, "Can there be any notion more repulsive, more violent, more dehumanizing than that of a wrathful god, as Paul calls him, who demands to be satisfied with an abhorrent torture of the human body and the shedding of its blood?" Such an entity cannot possibly be a god of reason and understanding. Nor can he be a god of justice, since justice does not depend upon savagery and death but upon reason.

Such a blood lusting and wrathful being is the stuff of myth, of nightmarish ancient fears, of humankind's darkest inclinations. We must raise ourselves to a new consciousness and leave behind such atavistic and primal notions. While Paul and the gospel writers worked from a world conception in which angry and jealous gods needed to be appeased by tasting the blood of their own creation, the fact that such notions still construct today's religious paradigm is not only unacceptable, it is an outrage against intellect and reason.

CHAPTER 7. RESURRECTION AND ASCENSION: "THE TRUMPET SHALL SOUND"

Paul's theological fabrications are not limited to the irrational concept of a blood lusting god and the notion of humankind's redemption from the fall of a mythical ancestor. For Paul, the doctrine of a blood sacrifice to expiate an imaginary sin has further implications. From his doctrine of redemption from sin by the death of the Jesus he never knew, Paul elaborates the subsequent notion of the resurrection. Paul first establishes the notion of the resurrection of Jesus and then extends this doctrine with the promise of a future resurrection of all humankind from the grave. Chapter 15 of Paul's first epistle to the Corinthians, in which he sets out the notion of the resurrection of Jesus and the resurrection of humankind, is a nothing short of the word-twisting of a con-artist salesman. To read these words uncritically or to hear these words pronounced might easily seduce and overwhelm the reader or listener in their kaleidoscopic and inundating rhetoric. Paul claims that the doctrine of the resurrection of the dead is the core of Christianity, yet, if we step back and look at this passage verse by verse and word by word, it has no logical or rational foundation. Paul declares:

> Now if Christ is preached as raised from the dead, how can some of you say that there is no resurrection of the dead? But if there is no resurrection of the dead, then Christ has not been raised; raised from the dead, how can some of you say that there is no resurrection of the dead? If Christ has not been raised, then our preaching is in vain and your faith is in vain. (1Corinthians 15:12–14)

The first consideration of this passage is the rather strange logic, or rather illogic, of its argument. The reasoning of the verses is so convoluted as to be almost impossible to break down for analysis. In short, what Paul is saying is that "the resurrection is true because I said it is." The first sentence has no foundation whatsoever. To "preach" that Christ is raised from the dead certainly does not mean that he *was* raised from the dead.

The second sentence is equally meaningless. The verse stumbles over its own words. It is devoid of logic. To contend that "if there is no resurrection of the dead, then Christ has not been raised; raised from the dead" requires that the speaker first establish that there is a resurrection from the dead, a premise that is, of course, impossible. If Paul has not at all proven that there is a resurrection, then indeed the answer to his own proposal is that Christ was not raised from the dead.

Furthermore, the rational reader might also respond to the last verse, "If Christ has not been raised, then our preaching is in vain and your faith is in vain." A simple response to Paul's assertion is that he has offered no proof whatsoever. And yes: if we accept that, if Jesus was not raised, then Paul's preaching is in vain — we would have to agree, "Yes, your preaching is indeed in vain as is your faith, because you have proven nothing and your idea of resurrection is based on something that not only did not happen but something that defies reason and the laws of nature." But as with so many florid biblical passages, the words of Paul's verses sound as though they should mean something, something of great importance. Only they don't. Indeed such verses that sound like something important are always appealing to bible thumpers and blind believers.[1]

Beyond Paul's convoluted reasoning, the notion of the bodily resurrection defies all rational thought. Yet, how many are the numbers of well-educated and otherwise thoughtful Christians who blindly embrace Paul's meaningless proclamations without the slightest doubt? They do not stop to consider that Paul's notion of a resurrection makes no more sense than his idea that at one time humankind did not know death: the doctrine upon which the invention of the resurrection is based. Furthermore, we must consider the kind of god that Paul envisions in his scheme. Paul's notions on the reason for death and the triumph of the resurrection suggest a god who is not only some kind of manipulative and manic puppeteer who creates and destroys, but he is one who has no sense of the economy of his own creation. What kind of god creates a living being only to destroy it and then to resurrect it? What purpose does such ambiguity serve? When Paul proposes elsewhere in 1 Corinthians, "The last enemy to be destroyed is death"(15:6), he reveals nothing more than wishful thinking. Furthermore, why should death be an enemy? Death is integral to the succession and evolution of all life.

---

[1] Take for example a cherished bible thumper verse, "'The Lord said to my Lord, Sit at my right hand, till I put thy enemies under thy feet'" Matthew 22:44, and its source Psalm 110.

Equally irrational in Paul's theology is the choice of time and place for humankind's redemption. Why, if this god wishes to recall all his creation to himself, does he send a redeemer only after hundreds of thousands of years of humankind's existence on earth? What of all the people who came before that time? We also then have to question why this redeemer should be sent only to a small tribe of people in one tiny place on the globe. These questions are so basic we have to wonder why they do not occur to most Christians. Yet, even as I put these questions in writing I am ashamed of my own gullibility to have never posed them before to my own self.

Even to ask such obvious questions and ponder them seems a trivial use of reason and intellect. These questions are so absurd as to belong with the medieval question of "how many angels can dance on the head of a pin?", or of children arguing at Christmastime about how Santa Claus comes into a house that has no chimney—when there are no angels or Santa Claus in the first place.

The hope of resurrection from death is sadly nothing more than myth creation. Would that resurrection and eternal life were possible; but such is simply not the case. For one thing, what would be its purpose? Why would we have been created into life and then subjected to death, only to be revived? Why would we have to wait for some unknown future time for this resurrection to take place? The earliest Christians, including Paul, expected this resurrection in their own lifetime. It never happened. It never happened because not only does the concept make no sense it has no possibility in reality.

This life is the only one we have. It doesn't have a rerun. Death is part of the process of the ever changing evolution of all life. It is nature's clearing of the slate generation after generation as the immense breadth and diversity of all things adjust, adapt and progress. Human life is no exception to that cycle. We must move beyond the mythic imagination that creates a world where we live forever and free ourselves to the reality of our fate. Death is not a state to be feared. In death there is no cognizance, no thought, no suffering, no bliss. Death is the simple, pure beauty of nothingness.

One of the most contrived of Paul's inventions is the notion of the return of Jesus to gather up the souls of the faithful. Christian fundamentalists and televangelists are more than fond of this event that they heatedly call "The Rapture."

> For the Lord himself will descend from heaven with a cry of command, with the archangel's call, and with the sound of the trumpet of God. And the dead in Christ will rise first; then we who are alive, who are left, shall be caught up together with them in the clouds to meet the Lord in the air; and so we shall always be with the Lord. (1 Thessalonians 4: 16–17)

Could there be any passage with more cataclysmic energy? This is the stuff of contemporary disaster films. It has all the drama and impact of the greatest epic. Yet, can there be any event more absurd? Passionate preachers delight in the images of sounding trumpets, angel's cries and the thundering voice of Jesus. Indeed, this scenario is one that such preachers seek to emulate in their tirades to gullible adherents who take no time to consider anything beyond the adrenaline excitement of hearing those verses ranted by a bible thumping zealot. Why does the average, theoretically educated Christian not take a moment to realize the simple physical cosmic absurdity of the second coming? To start with, the clouds are not the curtain that divides the earth from the divine. They are no more than condensed water vapor. How too does a physical entity, human or divine, suddenly appear out of the vastness of the universe? And why would heaven be interested in or require the accompaniment of a trumpet and the cry of angels? These are the elements of myth, of wonderful story telling, but they have no foundation in anything beyond the pleasures of the imagination.

How did Paul come to contrive his notion of the resurrection of the dead? We may never have a definitive answer to this question. Was he working from ancient notions already in place since the time of the Egyptians? Was Paul borrowing notions from Greco–Roman myth? Was he working from oral traditions about Jesus circulating at the time? Or, was this something he devised on his own? Any or all of the above are possible. The source of Paul's invention is not the issue. What can be said is that, just like Paul's notion of the fall of Adam, Paul not only defies reason but he also lacked scriptural substantiation for his promise of the resurrection of the dead.

Of course, when it comes to Paul's relationship to anything discussed in the gospels, we must bear in mind that the gospels date after Paul's epistles. Thus, just as with Paul's notion of Jesus as a blood sacrifice, Paul's ideas about the resurrection of Jesus do not depend on the gospel accounts. Quite to the contrary, the gospels' resurrection stories may have evolved from what Paul said. Then too, the resurrection story may also derive from an oral tradition that was already in various stages of its development and which Paul codified.

When looking at the story from a broader perspective, we cannot ignore the suppositions of those who contend that early Christianity was influenced by certain pagan traditions concerning the resurrection of a murdered god. There are those who would cite the Egyptians story of Osiris, who was destroyed by his rivals and then restored to life. They may also note the cult of Dionysius that celebrates the violent dismemberment of the god and his ultimate restoration. The element lacking from these tales and others like them is that none of them recounts a god who rises bodily from the dead. While such references may be titillating, and they are the stuff of great speculation,[1] I mention them only in attempt at completeness. But even if we set aside the ancient resurrection tales and apply ourselves only to Christian written accounts of the resurrection of Jesus, we find ourselves in a problematic situation in attesting to their veracity. Let us now turn to the reports of the resurrection as recounted in the gospels.

The source of Paul's notion of the resurrection may never be fully known. An equally intriguing question is the source of the gospel accounts. As any careful reader will note, the gospel accounts are quite diverse and show little consistency from one version to the other. This lack of consistency becomes all the more striking when we consider the absolutely spectacular nature of such an event. The gospel writers want to proclaim the restoration of a man from death to life. This event, at least as we have seen in Paul, will be the cornerstone of their faith. Yet, surely we can agree that if such an event actually took place, the reports of the first eyewitnesses would, by virtue of the immensity and impact of the event, have been close to identical. Yet, this is not at all the case. Not only do the accounts differ in minor details but they do not agree in significant elements.

They are not even consistent in who the witnesses were and what they saw. In Mark, the oldest gospel account, the women are identified as Mary Magdalene, Mary the mother of James, and Salome, "And when the Sabbath was past, Mary Magdalene, and Mary the mother of James, and Salome, bought spices, so that they might go and anoint him" (Mark 16:1). When the three women arrive at the tomb, the stone has already been rolled back and there is a young man inside who announces that Jesus has risen, "And looking up, they saw that the stone was rolled back;—it was very large" (Mark 16: 4–5).

In Matthew, the story becomes more dramatic. But in Matthew's account it is only Mary Magdalene and the "other" Mary who go to the tomb where, as the earth quakes, they encounter an angel who in radiant splendor rolls away the stone announces that Jesus has risen,

> Now after the Sabbath, toward the dawn of the first day of the week, Mary Magdalene and the other Mary went to see the sepulcher. And behold, there was a great earthquake; for an angel of the Lord descended from heaven and came and rolled back the stone, and sat upon it. (Matthew 28: 1–2)

When we turn to Luke's version, there seems to be a larger group of women, "The women who had come with him from Galilee followed, and

---

[1] The internet provides no small number of sites with a plethora of such claims. I would also note that such sites not only dazzle with their speculations but the sites themselves are usually fully loaded with what I might call visual extravagances.

saw the tomb, and how his body was laid" (Luke 23:55). When at the tomb, these women encounter not one man but two. Out of this group of Jesus' women followers from Galilee Luke identifies three in subsequent verses as Mary Magdalene, Joanna and Mary the mother of James. "Now it was Mary Magdalene and Joanna and Mary the mother of James and the other women with them who told this to the apostles" (Luke 24:10)[1].

In John, the last of the gospels to be written, the account is again quite different. In John it is Mary Magdalene alone who arrives at the tomb to find the stone rolled away. But she sees no angelic messengers nor experiences any earthquake. Mary makes a far more original encounter at the tomb. When she arrives, she finds that the tomb is empty. Thinking that the body has been stolen, she runs to Peter and John for help. The two men find the tomb empty except for the shroud and the face cloth. John tells us that while the two men "believed" they did not "understand" and simply returned home. At that point, Mary who is still at the tomb weeping, sees a man she believes to be the gardener and who turns out to be none other than Jesus himself (John 20 1–18).

The inerrancy of scripture is not the question here. That scripture can err is obvious in the multiple accounts of the resurrection. Clearly all the versions cannot all be correct. And so we find that we must ask how it is that such a remarkable event can have four variations. One of the only points that is consistent is that one of the principal witnesses was Mary Magdalene. What's more, in Mark, the oldest account, scholars and most bibles tell us that the oldest manuscripts did not have the ending of chapter 16 from verses 9 to 20. In the oldest manuscripts Mark brings his account toward its conclusion in verses 1 through 8 with the arrival of the women, the two Mary's and Salome, at the tomb where a young man (not an angel) greets them. He tells them that Jesus has risen and that he will meet them in Galilee. His final words advise the women to return to inform the disciples and Peter. Yet despite what they have been told to do by the young man, Mark's final words are, "And they [the women] went out and fled from the tomb; for trembling and astonishment had come upon them; and they said nothing to any one, for they were afraid"(Mark 16:8). There is something intriguing about the women's silence in this verse. Is Mark trying to forestall any doubts among his readers that Jesus actually did rise? By saying that the women told no one, is Mark lending a kind of mystery to the event? Is he protesting up front that the resurrection is veiled in a mystery that even the women who witnessed the empty tomb were frightened into silence? What

---

[1] See *Misquoting Jesus*, Ehrman, Bart D. New York: Harper, Collins, 2005 (Textual criticism of the last twelve verses) for a discussion on the possibility that Luke's resurrection story was added by a later writer.

is more, these women did not see Jesus at all but only the place where they had laid his body.

In the end we must ask, how could the discovery of an empty tomb, a body risen from the dead, and the details surrounding such a phenomenon not be clearly and distinctly impressed on the memory of the witnesses? Would the teller of the tale not at least be certain of who was there? If Peter and John were there, as John contends, would this not have been known to all, if not through others then from Peter himself?

Clearly, the resurrection tale is a narrative invention contrived by a group of emotionally invested followers of Jesus who sought to give meaning to their teacher's execution.[1] But the equivocation of the four evangelists' narratives is not the only problem with the resurrection story any more than the imaginative inventions of Paul's epistles. There is a far more rational and compelling consideration of such an event.

Beyond Paul and beyond the gospels the notion of a bodily resurrection itself defies all that is rational. The reason is quite simple and quite direct. All living creatures are destined to an end. They are destined to die. Through the death and end of each generation is the creation and continuation of the next. As we have noted, there was never a time when all livings things did not know death and there was never a time, nor will there ever be, a moment in history when life will be restored to all that has passed. Then, too, as already mentioned, why would a god create only to destroy then create again? It certainly doesn't seem to be a very rational process. Even in the most basic of physical terms, there are things here that give pause. Where would all the billions of physical bodies go? What purpose would they serve when resurrected? Even when taken in the context of the "end times" when the physical world will pass away it makes no sense. Why would we have a restoration of our physical bodies in the promised new realm where all that is physical has been swept away?

As we read in the second epistle of Peter, "But the day of the Lord will come like a thief, and then the heavens will pass away with a loud noise, and the elements will be dissolved with fire, and the earth and the works that are upon it will be burned up" (2 Peter 3:10).[2] The doctrine of a resurrection of

---

[1] While I have reservations about entering this note, I think it may provide a similar example. Those of a certain age will remember that after the death of Elvis Presley and the assassination of President Kennedy, there were numerous and constant reports that they were alive. Of course, the reports were highly charged emotionally and were completely fraudulent. Such reports, however, may have had historical antecedents in the death of Jesus.

[2] This epistle was clearly not written by Peter the apostle and its admission to the canon of scripture has always been questionable. Eusebius writes, "One epistle of Peter, that called the first, is acknowledged as genuine. And this the ancient elders used freely in their own writings as an undisputed work. But we have learned that his extant second Epistle does not belong to the canon; yet, as

the dead, however, does not limit itself to its own impossibility. The notion of the resurrection of Jesus led to the need to contrive yet another irrational doctrine that even more blatantly defies reason and understanding, the doctrine of the ascension of Jesus into heaven. Once the followers of Jesus had determined that Jesus was restored to life, they had to figure someway to account for the absence of the resurrected man who had vanquished death. If Jesus rose from the dead, where was he now? Why was he no longer among his followers? There could be only one solution to this problem. What to do but to send Jesus into the heavenly realm above the earth?

Once again, as we saw in the resurrection stories, the gospels have mixed accounts. In Mark's account, the oldest gospel, the earliest manuscripts do not contain an ascension story. Versus 9 through 20 of his final chapter 16 were later additions.[1] In Matthew's gospel, there is no ascension at all. Matthew concludes with some kind of ambiguous ending where Jesus gives his followers his last words on a mountain top in Galilee (Matthew 28: 16–20). The reader is left to wonder what becomes of Matthew's Jesus. There is, in Matthew, however, an intriguing set of verses that functions not unlike the silence of the women in Mark—insofar as they seem to suggest in advance and allay any possible doubt on the part of the reader. To dispose of the body, Matthew tells us the story of the guards who are paid off by the elders to explain the missing Jesus. "Tell people, 'His disciples came by night and stole him away while we were asleep' (Matthew 28:13). A rumor, Matthew tells us, which was being circulated at the time. "So they [the soldiers] took the money and did as they were directed; and this story has been spread among the Jews to this day" (28:15).

Matthew then tells his readers something rather odd, a little comment that seems to go unnoticed. Jesus has instructed his eleven remaining disciples to meet with him on a mountain in Galilee. But, "when they saw him they worshiped him; but some doubted" (28: 17). Who indeed were the ones who doubted and what was the cause of their doubt? If Jesus were standing in front of them and some worshiped him, what was questionable? Matthew seems a little uncertain himself. At this point he goes right into what is called "The Great Commission." His Jesus tells his followers, "Go and make disciples of all nations....And surely I am with you even to the end of the age." Of course, it must be said that the text of the great commission is generally considered a later addition to the gospel's otherwise abrupt conclusion. If we leave off that ending, Matthew's Jesus just ceases in the narrative thread. Does he go off into the mountains where he has called them together? Does he rise into the clouds? It seems rather strange that Matthew,

---

it has appeared profitable to many, it has been used with the other Scriptures." *Ecclesiastical History*, Book 3, Chapter 3.

[1] Most contemporary translations will make note of this addition.

who was careful enough at the start of his gospel to explain the very meaning of the name "Jesus," now simply concludes his gospel with no substantive ending.

To read a fuller and a clearer ascension account, we have to go to the master story teller, Luke. In his gospel version the ascension is rather simple. Luke tells his readers that Jesus took his followers out to Bethany where he blessed them and then was raised into heaven. "While he blessed them, he parted from them, and was carried up into heaven" (Luke 24:51).

It is when Luke reprises the ascension account in Acts that he offers a few more details, details that defy all we know of the physical universe. In both of Luke's accounts Jesus does not rise into heaven on his own, as the imagination may picture it. In Luke's gospel Jesus is "taken up into heaven" (24:51) and in Acts Jesus is carried up by a cloud.

> ...as they were looking on, he was lifted up, and a cloud took him out of their sight. And while they were gazing into heaven as he went, behold, two men stood by them in white robes, and said, "Men of Galilee, why do you stand looking into heaven? This Jesus, who was taken up from you into heaven, will come in the same way as you saw him go into heaven." (1:9–11)

Where can this Jesus possibly be going? How does a cloud carry away a human body? These questions appear foolish when put in writing, but they are founded on traditional and unquestioned Christian doctrine. In the mind of the ancient world such notions may be possible. Here we see again the ancient notion of the universe where a real and physical space above the clouds is the dwelling place of the divine. But how can such notions continue today?

John, the most highly philosophical of the evangelists is, like Matthew, silent on the subject. In his gospel, despite its otherwise metaphysical scenes there is no Ascension. The New Testament reader needs to go one book further than the four gospels to Acts to find yet another version where after speaking to his disciples and "as they were looking on, he was lifted up, and a cloud took him out of their sight (Acts 1:9). We must once again ask, would not such a marvelous event strike the witnesses with such force and wonder that they would have remembered it with greater singularity?

Curiously, Paul has little specifically to say on the actual event of the Ascension. The closest he comes to attesting to the ascent itself is in Ephesians 4:8: "Therefore it is said, "When he ascended on high he led a host of captives, and he gave gifts to men." Paul does, however, make repeated references to a Jesus who abides in heaven. We read, for example, in the epistle to the Thessalonians, of a Jesus ascended into a heaven where the saved will one day rise to meet him. "Then we which are alive and remain shall be caught up together with them in the clouds, to meet the Lord in the air: and so shall we ever be with the Lord" (1 Thessalonians 4:17). This miraculous event, the so called "Rapture" of Christian fundamentalists, pushes the irrational concept of life after death to its limit.

Once again, for the ancient world that believed in a god or gods who dwelt in the ethers above the earth, the idea of rising into the celestial sphere makes perfect sense. Where else would Jesus go but back to the realm of the one whom Christians thought to be his divine father? That realm was in the sky above, in that area of space beyond which the ancients called the firmament. For them, above that firmament, above that celestial dome that separated the earth from the heavens, there was another realm where the gods dwelt, overlooking and overseeing humankind. There, Jesus would wait, "seated at the right hand of power" until he returned "coming on the clouds of heaven" (Matthew 26:64). Such an image of Jesus encapsulates one of the most primitive notions of humankind, the notion of a of a sky god, a Zeus, a Jupiter reigning with vengeance on the inhabitants of the earth below.

In the ancient world the earth ruled at the center of the solar system. Above the earth were the heavens, the realm of the gods. These realms were sometimes described in distinct divisions. Writers from Cicero to Dante speak of the celestial spheres. Even Paul in 2nd Corinthians 12:2 tells us that he was raised to the sphere of the third heaven. Peter Apian's 1539 illustration shows us an interpretation of this notion.

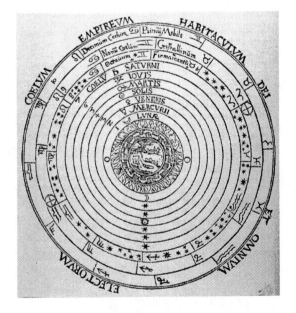

Geocentric celestial spheres; Peter Apian's Cosmographia *(Antwerp, 1539)*

This 16th century diagram of the universe clearly indicates the outmost ring, far beyond all other bodies of the celestial orbs, as the "habitaculum dei," the dwelling of god. From the most ancient times even up to the discoveries of Copernicus and Galileo, such a structured and organized view of the cosmos in distinct levels might be considered reasonable. In such a construction we might pass from one level to another. Indeed, in this pre-scientific arrangement of the heavens, the gods might descend to visit the earth and a human being might rise from the earth into one of the realms above. But this perception of the universe is clearly no longer acceptable. We know that this ancient notion is far from reality.

For the ancients, the notion that the gods reigned in the realm above the clouds may have been most plausible. One of the great moments in the cultural evolution of humankind was the development of a belief in the sky gods, gods who in the Greco–Roman world became the great Olympians and who among the Hebrews evolved into Yahweh. All these gods directed man from their celestial abode. Even after the passing of the pagan gods, the Christian god, along with his angels and saints, dwelled in the various levels of the heavenly spheres. Dante in his Divine Comedy charts their placement and assigns their hierarchy. Milton tells of the harmony of the universe that resonates from the interplay of those crystal spheres. All the imagery, all the poetry came to an abrupt end when one certain Galileo Galilei turned an optical glass towards the sky above and saw that there were no crystal spheres, no angelic choirs, no realm of the gods. Above the earth was space, endless space. As we know today Galileo observed only the smallest percentage of an infinite expanse of countless galaxies of countless stars: an infinity that does accommodate the risen physical body of any being in a heavenly paradise. In short, Jesus had no place to go. We know that this ancient notion is far from reality past or present. Yet, how many Christians weigh what they know about the universe against what they profess in church?

Thus, the question we must ask about this concept is: how do such primitive images, literal or metaphoric, still frame the religious ideas of contemporary Christians? How is it that early Christian notions of god sitting in judgment and calling before him all creation at the last trumpet still permeate Western culture as a whole? Paul writes, "In a moment, in the twinkling of an eye, at the last trumpet. For the trumpet will sound, and the dead will be raised imperishable, and we shall be changed" (1 Corinthians, 15:52). What notion could be more appealing, more intoxicating, more comforting to our mortal existence?

Painters, sculptors and composers have seized upon that cataclysmic moment to express their vision of its moment in some of the most dramatic and expressive creations in Western art. To cite but a few, the cathedrals Notre Dame, Chartres and Autun set above the heads of their entering congregations the horrors and wonders of the final trumpet blast. In the Renaissance we wonder in amazement before Michelangelo's *Last Judgment* in the Sistine Chapel. We shiver upon hearing Paul's words in Handel's intoxicating *Messiah*. We melt in submission upon hearing Mozart's *Lacrimosa*. We tremble at Verdi's *Requiem* and we dissolve on hearing Fauré's *In Paradiso*. Such masterpieces of Western art would not exist without the words of Paul and his epic of the fall of humankind and its redemption by the death and resurrection of his tragic hero, Jesus.

Paul's declaration and its many manifestations in the arts comfort us against the meaninglessness of life in the face of inevitable and terminal death. Yet, believing does not make it so. There is simply no reason at all to believe that those who have gone before us will one day rise from the dust to be reconstituted in a transformed universe. We will have lived our time on earth. We need not expect more.

Chapter 8. What Did Jesus Teach? "Blessed Are They"

"God is love": a simple statement that stands at the heart of Christian teaching, a teaching that stands apart from doctrine. But how did that notion develop? Who is responsible for the most fundamental sentiment to which Christians everywhere subscribe? Was it Jesus who first taught this precept? If so, which Jesus? The Jesus of Mark? The Jesus of John? The Jesus of Paul? It would seem that a more careful reading of biblical texts suggests that this teaching, as with many other Christian tenets, is not the direct product of Jesus but is a concept that developed and evolved over the first hundred years of Christianity.

The epistles or Paul, as we know, are the oldest New Testament scriptures. In the writing of Paul the notion of love is the most highly developed. Paul's first epistle, 1st Thessalonians is generally held to have been written around the year 50.[1] Mark, the oldest of the gospels, dates from sometime around the year 70, just after the destruction of the Temple. Thus, Mark, so close to Paul's early writings, would be the least influenced by his perspective, and so contains little mention of the love message. By the time of the writings of John, somewhere around the years 90 to 100, Paul is in his concluding years. His influence in the Christian community has produced a very clear vision. Thus John's, the latest gospel, is replete with notions of love for one another first developed by Paul. The reader who takes the time to carefully read Paul's epistles and the gospels in the historical context of their composition cannot fail to see the relationship and the development of distinct and individual points of view concerning the Christian concept of love for one another. The unprejudiced reader will soon see that there is not one monolithic Jesus message but several. The notion of love as

---

[1] Some scholars hold that Galatians may have been written around the same time or perhaps a bit earlier.

the foundation of Christian teaching may not be as clear cut in the teachings of Jesus as most may be given to believe.

In this chapter we ask, "What did Jesus actually teach? What was at the center of his message?" Can we ever really know the answer to these questions? At present, no. Perhaps, at some time in the future, if one day a manuscript is discovered that was written as a first-hand witness to the life and teachings of Jesus, we may have a picture that is a bit more clear. But, at present, no such manuscript is open to our view. We know Jesus only "through a glass darkly"(1 Corinthians 13:12) as he is presented in five differing versions: the gospels of Matthew, Mark, Luke and John and the epistles of Paul. Each presents a very distinct Jesus. We have to remember that all of the accounts of Jesus that we have were written well after his time. They were written in Greek, a language that Jesus did not speak. And in most cases, the gospels as we have them were written in places where Jesus never set foot. The gospels and the epistles were written by people who never knew him, who never saw him and never heard him. So, whatever the authors of the New Testament set in writing is less a record of actual events than a presentation of what each author wants his Jesus to do and say. How can we learn any kind of truth about who this man was and what he taught?

The teaching of love for one another is not so central to the earliest Jesus accounts. To see how the teaching of brotherly love evolves, we have to move with the dates of each gospel's creation. If we start with Mark as a base-line gospel, we can easily see the development of this essential teaching on love. We find that a simple statistical count of the number of times we find the word "love"[1] [2] in the gospels can be quite telling. As we progress from the earliest gospel text, Mark, and then on through to Matthew, then Luke and finally John, we find a distinct and measurable increase in the use of the word "love." In Mark, the earliest extant version, the word "love" is found only three times. The Jesus of Matthew uses the word nine times but only in six of these passages use the word as an instruction. As we progress to the wonderful literature of Luke, Jesus speaks the word ten times, five of which are instructive. And by the time we finish at John, Jesus pronounces this word no fewer than twenty-two times, nearly all of which are as a teaching. We see in this evolution the ever increasing influence of Paul's epistles. When we look at Mark we find only one passage where his Jesus speaks of love. His

---

[1] "God is love, and he who abides in love abides in God, and God abides in him" (1 John, 4:16). The authorship of this epistle is uncertain. Certain elements in its language suggest that it may not be the same person who wrote the gospel of John. It dates from well after the year 100 and would have been influenced by the post Pauline elements discussed in this chapter.

[2] I am counting only the word "love" that translates from the Greek "ἀγάπη" "agape," that is "love" in its fullest meaning in relation to people, not the Greek "φιλία" (filia) which is used more for things and translates better as "like."

statement is not presented as novel teaching but in a direct response to the scribes who ask him which of the laws is the most important.

> And you shall love the Lord your God with all your heart, and with all your soul, and with all your mind, and with all your strength: The second is this, 'You shall love your neighbor as yourself.' There is no other commandment greater than these and to love him with all the heart, and with all the understanding, and with all the strength, and to love one's neighbor as oneself, is much more than all whole burnt offerings and sacrifices." (Mark, 12:30–33)

For Mark's Jesus, these are neither original words nor an original thought. Mark's Jesus is simply quoting Deuteronomy and Leviticus.[1] For this Jesus, the notion of love for God and for neighbor is the simple keeping of the given Law of Moses. Mark's Jesus is teaching nothing new. Furthermore, Mark's rendition of this teaching is notable for what it does not contain. It does not clarify just who is intended by "neighbor." The author of Luke is aware of this oversight. In Luke, the question does not end as matter-of-factly as it does in Mark. In Luke, Jesus' questioners then ask him, "Who is my neighbor?" This is a simple question but one that reveals a significant development in the image of Jesus. Thus, Luke's Jesus goes a step beyond the Jesus of Mark. In Luke, Jesus immediately follows with the fully developed parable of the Good Samaritan.[2] In this tale a neighbor is not simply someone whom we know. In this tale, we learn that a neighbor is that very person whose race and background in our ignorance we consider as outcast and unacceptable. But as we have seen in Mark, the earliest text, this refinement is not yet in the consciousness of the narrator. Indeed, when we look at Mark, we find a story that gives a very different picture of who his Jesus sees as a neighbor. For Mark's Jesus, one's neighbor was probably just that, those people of your own kind and vicinity. In Mark, Jesus' very own reaction to a non-Jew, an outsider, is nothing less than disdainful. When the woman of foreign birth approaches Jesus to ask him to dispel a demon who possesses her daughter, Mark's Jesus has little empathy for her as a neighbor. In fact, he ranks her among the lowest of creatures and calls her a dog. "Let the children first be fed, for it is not right to take the children's bread and throw it to the dogs" (Mark 7:27).

Yet another example in Mark where his Jesus seems little interested in the concept of love for one another is the story of the Rich Young Man. When the rich young man approaches Jesus to ask, "What must I do to inherit eternal life?" Mark's Jesus replies by noting the importance of following the laws of Moses, "Do not kill, do not commit adultery, do not steal, do not bear false witness, do not defraud, honor your father and mother" (Mark 10:25).

---

[1] Leviticus 19:18. Deuteronomy 6:5.
[2] Luke 10: 30-37.

While Jesus then tells the young man to sell all he has and give it to the poor, the concern seems more for the danger of riches than for the wellbeing of the poor. This Jesus of Mark, in this story, does not at all mention the idea of love for one's fellows as a requisite in and of itself.

It would seem that the Jesus of Mark is not overly concerned with love for one another. Mark's Jesus is a wonder worker who cures the ill and the possessed: "And he healed many who were sick with various diseases, and cast out many demons" (Mark 1:34). Indeed, the first miracle of Mark's Jesus is the exorcism of a demon (Mark 1: 21–27).Then, in an impressive sequence of wondrous acts, Mark's Jesus is occupied with cure after cure. Mark's Jesus is an incomparable wonder worker. Nowhere does Mark's Jesus speak on the importance of brotherly love. The Jesus of Mark never gives the Sermon on the Mount. He has no words about mercy or peace or humility.[1] This early Jesus does not impart the simplicity of the Lord's Prayer[2] or suggest (as will a later gospel) that "'Truly, I say to you, as you did it to one of the least of these my brethren, you did it to me" (Matthew, 25:40). Mark's Jesus does not set before his listeners the example of the Good Shepherd (John 10:11) and never utters the admonition to "love one another," as the Jesus of John does repeatedly.[3]

Even when we consider closely those passages that may seem to attest to a Jesus who shows a certain affection, such as the admonition to "Let the children come to me," we note that the purpose is to compare them to those who will inherit the "kingdom of heaven" (Mark, 19:13–14). Further still, when it comes to family and children, Mark's Jesus shows no concern for familial love. For this Jesus, "everyone who has left houses or brothers or sisters or father or mother or children or lands, for my name's sake, will receive a hundredfold, and inherit eternal life" (Mark, 19: 29).

The gospel of Mark, the text that in all likelihood portrays Jesus the most accurately in terms of his actual life and words, does not portray the Jesus that many Christians would describe. This is a Jesus who is not entirely personable and loving. This is a Jesus who has a somewhat different agenda.

In Mark, the mission of Jesus is that of a healer and a proclaimer of the coming kingdom of god. Yet, curiously he is one who also admonishes his followers not to speak of his wonder works. This Jesus is equally enigmatic when he often presents his listeners with hidden or secret sayings, a strange practice for one who supposedly wishes to reveal truths. His mission is that of a healer and preacher who, after he has performed a wonder, commands his followers to tell no one about it. Most important, however, this Jesus is intent upon proclaiming the coming of a kingdom. Indeed, the proclamation

---

[1] Matthew 5: 5.
[2] Matthew 6:9.
[3] John 13:34, 15:12, 15:17.

of this coming kingdom may very well be his primary message. And for this Jesus, this kingdom was imminent. More important, it would be one where he would rule and where his disciples would be his princes.[1] The Jesus of Mark was not a Jesus of love. Love is of little concern to this early version of Jesus. The notion of love for one another will only become more important in later texts: texts in all probability influenced in no small measure by the writings of Paul.

Not until we come to the gospel of Matthew, composed sometime after Mark, do we start to see a Jesus who has some concept of the notion of brotherly love. By the date of Matthew's gospel, it was already becoming questionable that the kingdom of God was immediately at hand as Mark's Jesus suggested. By this time too, Paul's teachings would have been gaining greater ground, particularly in the Gentile world. By the time Paul is writing, Jesus had been dead for quite some time and clearly Jesus had not established the kingdom as envisioned in Mark's gospel. Paul amends the prediction of Mark's earthly kingdom by transforming it into a kind of semi-spiritual kingdom. But for Paul, as with the Jesus of Mark, that kingdom is again imminent—except that in Paul that kingdom has become more metaphysical than that of Mark.

Equally important, Paul creates a new view of Jesus. He creates a Jesus who teaches the merits of love for one another. Yet, oddly, Paul's epistles quote not a word of any of the passages on love that are found in any the gospels. Indeed, Paul never quotes a word from Jesus except for the passage on the words of the Eucharist, a passage that Paul probably invented. With Paul's notion of a spiritual kingdom and his proclamations on brotherly love, Paul's influence touches the formation of the later gospels.

It is Matthew's Jesus who begins to make the turn that more closely approaches the teachings of Paul. Matthew's Jesus uses the word "love" nine times. It is Matthew's Jesus who preaches the Sermon on the Mount and who proclaims what many present day Christians hold as essential to the practice of their faith.[2] It is also in Matthew that we first learn the words of the "Lord's Prayer." Matthew's Jesus seems a bit more kind-hearted than Mark's Jesus. But, do not think that the more aggressive nature of Mark's Jesus is absent in Matthew. Matthew's gospel echoes elements of the Jesus who will bring discord.

> Do not think that I have come to bring peace on earth; I have not come to bring peace, but a sword. For I have come to set a man against his father, and a daughter against her mother, and a daughter-in-law against her mother-in-law; and a man's foes will be those of his own household. (Matthew 10:34–36)

---

[1] We will discuss this aspect in Chapter 8.
[2] Matthew 5:1-11.

Even Mark's Jesus does not speak of such an imminent disruption of family life in preparation for his coming kingdom of God.

We now turn to the writings of Luke to find yet another face to the Jesus of the gospels. Sometime just after the year 70, converts to Paul's religion may have been a minority cult but they were widespread in Asia Minor, Greece and even Italy. We find that Luke's Jesus is addressing a Greek-speaking audience, an audience that would have been familiar with the writings of Paul.

Luke's gospel, written either close to the time of Matthew or shortly thereafter, introduces a Jesus who may not specifically use the term "love" but whose parables are unique in the four gospels for their demonstration of love and kindness and concern for others. It is in Luke alone that Jesus explains the power of fatherly love and forgiveness in the parable of the Prodigal Son (15: 11–32). In the stories of the Lost Drachma (15:8–10) and the Lost Sheep (15:1–7), we read of those who do their utmost to retrieve the lost. The Jesus of Luke is all the more striking since these parables that teach love for all humankind fly in the face of the rather self-centered Greco–Roman world of the time: the world for whom Luke was writing his gospel. In that classic world of Luke's audience, it was the powerful hero, the Pius Aeneus of Virgil, the Achilles of Homer, who stood as the model to be emulated. In his gospel, Luke's Jesus resets the paradigm.

Catacombs of Priscilla c. 350, fresco.   *The Good Shepherd, 19th century stained glass. First Presbyterian Church, Delavan, IL.*

In keeping with Luke's skill as writer, his Jesus does not overtly preach his message with commands or threats. Luke's Jesus teaches tenderly by example, the example of his parables. (Curiously, this is not unlike our contemporary approach of teaching values to children where narrative modeling replaces didactic precepts.) Indeed, it is the Jesus of Luke, even more than the didactic Jesus of John, who embodies the Jesus most Christian would have in mind. We see this embodiment in a very real and physical way. Even in the arts, the image of Jesus carrying the lost sheep across his shoulders is not only one of the earliest depictions of Jesus but continues in our time as one of the most often reproduced in stained glass versions, particularly in Protestant churches.

Perhaps the most famous parable, a story whose very name is part of common vocabulary, is that of The Good Samaritan (10: 29–37). The Jesus of the parable sees all humankind as brothers and sisters. Indeed, this parable speaks across the ages into our own time. As you will recall, it is the Samaritan, the outcast of the majority society, who alone takes pity on the man who has been beaten and robbed. Most significant, however, is that this parable, as well as those others which Luke alone creates, do not propose rules like the quotation from Leviticus. They are not proclamations or promises as we read in the Beatitudes. They are not warning as we read in the story of the Rich Young Man. In these parables Luke has created a practical Jesus, a Jesus who offers clear and earthbound examples of thoughtful human behavior. While Luke may have built his gospel on the foundation of Mark's earlier text, Luke has endowed his Jesus with a fuller human quality: a Jesus with a sense of human needs. But Luke's contribution is not the last in the development of the Jesus of the gospels. Luke's worldly Jesus, will contrast sharply with the next Jesus to appear in the gospel of John.

Years pass for the early followers of the Jesus movement. The environment changes. The followers among the Gentiles have increased; the original Jewish community is a dispersed minority. Jerusalem has been laid waste by the Romans.[1] The imminent kingdom of god that Mark's Jesus preached is clearly not yet at hand. Paul's epistles have all been written and almost everyone who may have been witnesses to Jesus have since died. Christianity has moved almost exclusively into the Greek-speaking world of the Empire.

The gradual evolution of the Jesus of the gospels moves into its most Hellenized state. The simple preacher and wonderworker of Mark, the prophet of Matthew and the parable teller of Luke develop into a philosophical teacher who speaks in metaphors for the enlightened to comprehend. Somewhere around the year 100,[2] we leave behind the writings of the synoptic gospels and open the pages of the last of the accepted canonical gospels, the

---

[1] While not all scholars agree that Luke was written after the destruction of the temple in 70 AD, it would seem from Luke's "prediction" of the temple destruction (Luke 21: 5-6) that the gospel would have to date after this time.

[2] It must be said that, since John does not mention the destruction of the temple in the year 70, the text must date before that time. Yet, it must also be noted that there is little in John that seems to concern itself with actual historical events.

gospel of John. Like the eagle, the iconographic symbol that represents John's gospel, this text soars above the other three. While the synoptic gospels may have at least a minimal element of historicity, John is certainly almost pure invention. John's gospel is something of a philosophical exposition. The Jesus of John is the Greek "logos," the metaphysical incarnation of word and light. The Jesus of this gospel is nothing less than the worker of metaphoric miracles. He changes water to wine and raises the three day dead from the grave: miracles unknown to the Jesus of the synoptics.

While John's gospel may be a text comprised almost exclusively of metaphor and metaphysical language, it is also the only gospel whose Jesus is primarily concerned with teachings on brotherly love, teachings that seem to derive directly from the teachings of Paul. By the time of John's composition, which dates from about the year 100, the Christian world that was now almost fully divorced from the Jewish community where it originated. John's audience is Hellenic.

It is John's Jesus whose teachings eventually take hold of the Christian imagination and color the popular notion of the Jesus of the synoptics. In fact, it could be said that John's Jesus teachings on love are such that they mask the very different individual teachings of the earlier three gospels.

John's gospel is the source of several of the most famous passages on love including, "God is love, and he who abides in love abides in God, and God abides in him"(John 4:16), and "Greater love has no man than this that a man lay down his life for his friends"(John 15:13). None of these verses is known to the Jesus of the synoptics. Perhaps the passage on love that is most striking is this: "A new commandment I give to you, that you love one another; even as I have loved you, that you also love one another" (John 13:34).Compare this verse to the passage in the synoptics where Jesus is questioned about which commandment is the first of all. The Jesus of the synoptics responds by quoting Leviticus 19:18, "You shall love the Lord your God with all your heart, and with all your soul, and with your whole mind" (Matthew 22:37, Mark 12:30, Luke 10:27). John's Jesus, however, does not seem to be aware that the teaching of love for one's neighbor is already found in scripture. John's Jesus seems to think that he proclaims a novel idea. John's Jesus claims that he is giving "a new commandment."

Did Jesus actually pronounce the verses on love that are found in John? If he did, Mark's Jesus didn't know them; neither did the Jesus of Matthew or Luke. The Jesus of John, even when we leave aside his metaphysical language, is a Jesus who is speaking the language of Paul's epistles. So, who is this Jesus that today's Christians revere and hold as the teacher of brotherly love? A close investigation of the gospel texts clearly suggests that the Jesus of love never existed. If we are to attribute the teaching of love for one another to anyone, it should not be to Jesus, but rather to Paul. So, here again, as with the notion of the Eucharist, it is Paul who has invented the religious structure.

This invention that has called on us to love our enemy, to embrace our neighbor, to value one another as distinct individuals has been the foundation of our civilization. These are all teachings. They are not doctrines. While Christian doctrines may often have been the source of great conflict and even evil, the eventual good of Christian teaching has outweighed the greatest shortcomings. Truth be told, despite his irrational doctrinal propositions, we must also acknowledge that Paul has given us a new ethic. Christianity emerges as the inspiration of an unusual man, a tent maker from Tarsus, whose personal reasons for his teachings may never fully be known. The person of the historical Jesus serves only as a kind of dramatic mask, a "persona" that speaks according to the need of Paul's developing script.

Chapter 9. Crucifixion: "Hail King of the Jews"

> Then one of them, named Cleopas, answered him, "Are you
> the only visitor to Jerusalem who does not know the things that
> have happened there in these days?" And he said to them, "What
> things?" And they said to him, "Concerning Jesus of Nazareth,
> who was a prophet mighty in deed and word before God and all
> the people, and how our chief priests and rulers delivered him up
> to be condemned to death, and crucified him. But we had hoped
> that he was the one to redeem Israel. Yes, and besides all this, it is
> now the third day since this happened." (Luke 24: 18–21)

In the previous chapter I have proposed that the gospels do not present a
single and unilateral view of what Jesus taught. As demonstrated in Chapter 7,
the Jesus of Mark has little in common with the Jesus of Luke or Matthew, and
the Jesus of John has clearly nothing in common with the Jesus of the synoptics.
We also saw that the notion of Jesus as the teacher of brotherly love is certainly
not consistent but is rather a gradual development. Then, in addition to the
gospels, there is the Jesus of Paul who, never having known Jesus, seems to
have created something quite different altogether. When human reason and a
careful examination of scripture reveal these various portraits of Jesus, each with
a distinct agenda, created by five different writers, we come to the speculative
question, "Who did *Jesus* think he was?" Is there any way we might find some
common thread in the New Testament that will offer some suggestion?

Although I stated in the preface of this book that I was not interested in
pointless speculation about the historical Jesus, there is one question that I find
highly perplexing. I allow myself to present this question primarily because

its implications loom over my fundamental question of Jesus' death as an appeasing sacrifice to a blood-demanding god. I have set out most emphatically that the notion of Jesus as a blood sacrifice is completely implausible and contrary to reason in the post Enlightenment world. Yet, if indeed there was an historical Jesus who was crucified in accordance with Roman law, as the gospels claim, what then might have been the meaning and cause of his death? Do the gospel accounts suggest an answer either knowingly or unwittingly?

As we have attempted to show in this study, there is little to explain the death of Jesus rationally as a sin redemption. The notion of Jesus as a sacrifice to a blood-demanding god is an affront to all reason. From a scriptural point of view, the doctrine of the death of Jesus upon the cross as a redemption from the sins of mythical ancestors is founded upon clear misreadings and misinterpretations of earlier biblical texts. We then must ask if there is not some rational and perhaps historical reason for the arrest and execution of this itinerant preacher of Israel.

Why was Jesus executed? Why was he crucified? It may very well be that the gospels, even without the awareness of their authors, in a kind of "between the lines" testimony, give us the answer. These silent hints provoke several questions. Was Jesus executed on the cross for justifiable political reasons? Did Jesus actually think he was a king? Did he see himself as the long awaited messiah, the anointed one, who would free the Jews from their Roman occupiers? While the Jesus of the New Testament has many faces, there is one feature that each depiction of Jesus seem to have in common. Jesus saw himself as some kind of king.

Yet, before we can consider the question of Jesus' possible self-styled kingship, we need to take a little time on questions of language: an investigation that will strongly influence our conclusions. We must first carefully consider two words, or names, and how they are used in the scriptures, Old Testament and New. These two words, or names, are "Jesus" and "Christ." These two terms are almost always found together in the common parlance of today's Christian. They are used the way we use a person's first and last name. Indeed, there is probably no small number of people who assume that is exactly what they are: Jesus, his first name, and Christ his last name.

But each name tells us something quite distinct and quite revealing: things that time and usage have almost completely obscured. We need to ask two very simple questions that are usually not given a moment's thought. We must ask why was Jesus called "Jesus," and why was he called "Christ?"

First, we consider the name "Jesus." The name "Jesus" derives from the Hebrew "Yehoshua," (הֵיֹשׁוַע), or in its shorter form, "Yeshua."[1] Briefly explained, Yeshua is composed of two other words: the term "YHWH", (Yahweh), the mystical name of god, and the word "shua," meaning a cry to be saved. Set together, the name may be translated as "god saves."[2] More commonly, the name conveys the idea of "savior." In the Old Testament, the name is found as "Joshua." Yet, in the strange and often convoluted process of translation and transliteration, particularly by the early church fathers, a distinction was made that would clearly isolate the name of the New Testament "Jesus" and remove him from any association with the Joshua of the Old Testament.

The process may have gone something like this. The first step in the transition from the Hebrew "Yeshua" to our current "Jesus" is one of transliteration. For the most part, there is a one-to-one correspondence of the Hebrew sounds into Greek until you come up against the "sh" (שׁ) sound, for which Greek does not have an exact match. So, the translators of the Septuagint and then the authors of the gospels used the next closest sound, a simple "s." In addition to the "sh" to "s" change, Greek also had to give the name a masculine ending. To do that, the Greek adds the final "s." The result is a new name, "Iysous."

Now we must note that this is the same as the transliteration for the Old Testament name "Joshua." In other words, both Jesus and Joshua are written as "Iysous" (Ἰησοῦς). We might compare for example two passages, one from the Old Testament Septuagint, the other from the New Testament Greek. They read each, "Jesus said to them" and "Joshua said to them." (The word order is somewhat reversed. The Greek reads "and said to them Jesus".)

καὶ εἶπεν | αὐτοῖς	| ὁ Ἰησοῦς	
kai eipen | autois	| o Iysous	(Matthew 9:15)

καὶ εἶπεν | (πρὸς) αὐτοὺς	| Ἰησοῦς	
kai eipen | (pros) autous	| Iysous	(Joshua 10:25)[3]
and said | *to them*	| *Iysous*	

---

[1] *The Hebrew Names Bible* uses "Yehoshua" for Joshua and "Yeshua" for Jesus. Remember, however, that the use of "Yeshua" for the Greek "Iysous" is somewhat arbitrary since there is no Hebrew or Aramaic version of the New Testament.

[2] The exact derivation of the name "Yehoshua" is a study unto itself. This more than simplified etymology, however, is sufficient to define our consideration here.

[3] The only difference in the two verses is that Matthew uses the dative "autois" (to them), and the Septuagint uses the preposition "pros" with the accusative "autous" (to or towards them).

The names are identical in Greek: "Iysous," in both cases. It is only when we come to the Latin text translated by Jerome in the fourth century that a distinction between the two names is made.

For the Old Testament, Jerome, writing in Latin, transliterates Joshua as "Iosue." But when he comes to the New Testament, Jerome creates not just a transliteration from the Hebrew and the Greek but a distinctly new name, "Iesus." Not only does Jerome distinguish Jesus from Joshua, but in so doing he creates a new and distinct person in the scriptures. In this way the Jesus of the New Testament defines himself not only by what he does and says as does did Joshua, but by his unique name.

The essential point, however, is with this distinct transliteration into a new name Jerome completely removes the fuller meaning of the word, "Yehoshua." When most of us read or hear the name "Jesus"[1] as Jerome transliterated it, we hear only a personal name without its Hebrew denotation. When we read or hear the name "Jesus," we neither read nor hear a subtler meaning. More important, we do not hear how this appellation may have been used in the time of Jesus.

To understand the name "Jesus" as intended, we turn to the gospel of Matthew. There is some thought that Matthew was originally written not in Greek, like the other gospels, but in Hebrew.

> There is an ancient tradition going back to Eusebius (260–340) that the author of Matthew originally wrote in Hebrew. "These things are related by Papias ... concerning Matthew he writes as follows: "So then Matthew wrote the oracles in the Hebrew language and every one interpreted them as he was able." (Eusebius, *Writings of Papias*, Chapter XXXIX, v. 15–16)

While there is considerable question as to whether the Matthew of Eusebius is the same Matthew of the gospel, the fact remains that only Matthew takes the time to translate the meaning of the name Jesus from Hebrew into Greek. In Matthew we find the hidden subtleties which we are otherwise missing in the common understanding of the name "Jesus."

In the Matthew version of the nativity story, an angel speaks to Joseph in a dream. Joseph, who has been betrothed to Mary, discovers that she is pregnant. Joseph, knowing that he is not the father, contemplates divorcing Mary. Then:

> As he considered this [*the divorce*], behold, an angel of the Lord appeared to him in a dream, saying, "Joseph, son of David, do not fear to take Mary your wife, for that which is conceived in her is of the

---

[1] In the simplest terms, the "J" of English and some other languages devolves from a later Latin as the "yuh" sound shifts to a "juh" sound. The causes of this palatalization are another study beyond the scope of this text.

Holy Spirit; she will bear a son, and you shall call his name Jesus, for he will save his people from their sins." (Matthew 1:20–21)

If we were to read that name in its original language, we would have caught the fuller meaning. We would read something like, "You shall call his name 'God saves,' for he will save his people from their sins." With the reading of "God Saves" rather than "Jesus," the verse make much more sense. We get the play on words.

Now whether the account of Eusebius is correct or not, it would seem that the author of the Matthew gospel did indeed have an understanding of Aramaic and Hebrew. Furthermore, Matthew is considered by most biblical scholars to be the most Jewish of the gospels. He is, after all, also the only one who is attuned to the significance of the name "Yehosua" (Jesus) as verse 1:21 indicates. Yet, while the author of Matthew may have himself been attuned to the subtleties of the Hebrew, there is nothing for the Greek readers of his time or for today's readers of contemporary languages to see how the angel's explanation "for he will save his people" has anything to do with the name "Jesus." Unless the reader is specifically attuned to the Hebrew, there is nothing that clearly states that the name "Jesus" itself means "savior."

In contrast to Matthew's gospel, we consult Luke, the only other gospel with the Annunciation sequence. In Luke we do not see any explanation of the name. Luke's gospel, written by a Greek for a Greek audience, does not seem to be aware of this play on words. When Luke's Gabriel makes his announcement to Mary he proclaims, "And behold, you will conceive in your womb and bear a son, and you shall call his name Jesus. He will be great, and will be called the Son of the Most High; and the Lord God will give to him the throne of his father David" (Luke 1:31–32). Luke makes no mention of any connection between the name and its original Hebrew meaning. Luke was writing from a Greek foundation.[1]

Now, it also must be said that the name "Jesus" (or Joshua) was not uncommon in the time of the gospels. The name can be found elsewhere in the New Testament and in the histories of Josephus. In Acts, Paul and Barnabas encounter a magician by the name of Elymas bar-Jesus (Acts 13: 6). In Colossians, Paul speaks of one Jesus Justus (Colossians 4:11). Flavius Josephus tells of a Jesus, who like the one of the gospels was scourged by the Romans for his loud outcries against the city of Jerusalem. Also, like the Jesus of the gospels, this Jesus never spoke a word in his defense despite having his bones laid bare by the whipping. Unlike the Jesus we read in the gospels however, the Jesus in the writings of Josephus was not executed but was eventually released as a mad man (Wars of the Jews, Book 6, Chapter 5,

---

[1]   This translational transition is not unlike how the term "Christos" or "Anointed" moves from a general term to a specific nominative. I will discuss this immediately.

Part 3). These are but a few characters in history that share the same name. Archeologists and historians tell us that there were many more in that time period who carried the name "Jesus."

Yet, here is the difference. When Josephus speaks of a person by the name of Jesus, the person's name does not necessarily reflect the person's life or the role that person plays in the account. The same is true of the other Jesus persons mentioned in Acts (13:6) or Colossians (4:11). In these cases, the name is nothing more than a name. There are no connotations that associate the person's name with what he does. When, however, we look at the significant uses of the name of Joshua in the Old Testament and Jesus in the New, we see that this case is different. Joshua and Jesus are not only their names, they are also the roles that each of them plays. Just as Joshua led his armies against the enemies of the Hebrews in the Promised Land, so too was Jesus to lead his people against the Romans: an event which will be discussed shortly. Both Joshua and Jesus were saviors. Thus, in the case of Joshua and in the case of Jesus, the names are what we might call "attributive" names, that is, names that tell not who a person is but what a person does: the role that is played.

For the sake of what may be a clearer example, let me side track for a moment from biblical texts to the writings of the Middles Ages. In the hagiographic (saints' lives) writings of this period, we find no small number of heroic figures whose names were really so not much personal names as they were attributes or indicators of the person's actions or functions. One of the most famous is the name "Christopher." Take a moment to review his story. According to most versions of the legend, Christopher was a giant who carried the Christ child on his shoulders across a stormy and turbulent river. Now, if we look at the meaning of the name "Christopher," we quickly note that the name is derived from two Greek words: "Χριστός" (Christos), that is, "Christ," and the verb "φέρειν" (ferein), "carry." So, the name "Christopher" literally means "Christ carrier." His name is precisely the thing that he does. The name Christopher is not a name independent of the actions of the person, but rather, a name that illustrates the very thing that the person is known for: in this case, carrying Christ.[1]

Another striking example is the tale of Saint Veronica. The legend of Veronica tells us that she was among the women weeping for Jesus as he carried his cross through the streets of Jerusalem to Calvary. Taking pity on the suffering man, she wiped his face with her veil. When she opened the cloth, there, imprinted on its surface, was the face of Jesus. The name Veronica, however, is not a proper name but a descriptive that is a blending

---

[1] In 1969, the Roman Church, realizing that Christopher was clearly not a person but a concept, removed Christopher from the list of acknowledged saints.

of the words "verus" and "ikon" which is to say "true image." "Veronica" is not personal name, it is a descriptive name.[1]

Hans Memling c. 1470

The same "name equals function" is true for various other early Christian saints who may well have been mythical. Saint Faith, whose spectacular golden idol reliquary is in Conques, Southern France, offers a typical example. Sainte Foie, Saint Faith, is a saint whose name clearly refers to a quality and not to a person.[2] Or Saint Lucy (Sancta Lucia), who plucked out her own eyes rather than lose her virginity, which is a reference to what she has done. She has given up earthly light for heavenly light.

Sainte Foie, c. 10th century with earlier and later components.

Why do I offer these medieval references?[3] Because just as the names of these saints were not the names of actual persons but rather attributes of what the person did, so too we find the same type of naming in the scriptures. Just as Christopher is the "Christ carrier," so too is the Joshua (God saves) of the Old Testament the savior of his people as they enter the Promised Land. So too in the New Testament, Jesus (God saves) seeks to save his people, as their king, in a failed attempt against Roman rule. In each

---

[1] It must be noted that there is also another earlier meaning of the name. Eastern sources find that the name Veronica is a Latin variation of the Greek "Berenike" (Βερενίκη) meaning "carry victor").

[2] Saint Faith (Sainte Foye) has a remarkable shrine in the Southern French village of Conques. Her reliquary is a spectacular gem-encrusted gold image assembled, oddly enough, from the bust of a late Roman emperor.

[3] Fairy tales and folk tales offer even more examples. The principal characters in "Beauty and the Beast" have no actual names. Their names are their attributes. The same is true of "Sleeping Beauty."

case, the names seem less an indifferent personal appellation than a specific description of their narrative function. So, here is the question. Might the same situation apply to Jesus? Was "Jesus" the actual birth name of the man the gospels attempt to describe, or, like the Joshua of the Old Testament and certain saints of the Middle Ages, was his name not a name but an attribute, a description of what he did?

In other words, did the man the gospels call Jesus actually have a different birth name? Did this wandering prophet, taken by his own notions of what he was, choose to dub himself with the name? Did he see himself as the one who would "save his people" and so took on the telling name "Jesus"? Or, perhaps the name was given to him by his followers: followers like James and John who, as we shall discuss momentarily, believed he was going to establish a new kingdom here on earth? After all, such second naming is quite common in the New Testament. Simon was called Peter, the "rock." Saul was called Paul, the "small." Matthew is also Levi; Jesus calls James and John Boanerges [1] "sons of thunder," and Thomas is also Didymus, the "twin."

There is yet another curious clue about Jesus being called Jesus: the way in which his name is used by Jesus' followers. In short, it isn't. At no time in any of the gospel accounts does any of his immediate disciples or family address Jesus by name. While the crowds may address Jesus as "Lord," or "Master," or "Rabbi," they never address him by his supposed first name. The name "Jesus" occurs only in the third person as the subject of the narrative. There is only one exception, found only in Matthew and Luke. The only time Jesus is addressed as "Jesus" is when the blind man calls out to him, "Jesus, Son of David, have mercy on me!" (Matthew 10:47, Luke 18:38). And this address in the second person can easily be read not as a personal name but as an attributive name, particularly in Matthew. Take a moment to reread that cry for help with the actual meaning of "Jesus." Replacing the proper name "Jesus," with the meaning of the name we read, "*Savior*, Son of David, have mercy on me!" With this substitution, the name "Jesus" has a very different complexion, particularly when coupled with the phrase, "Son of David," which is to say, the promised king of Israel. The name Jesus is always found in a way where when we substitute the personal name "Jesus" with its function, "Savior," we begin to read something quite different. We begin to see a story that more resembles such tales as those of Joshua in the Old Testament, the "savior" of his people, or of something like the medieval Christopher who carried Christ across the raging river. The name, Jesus (Yehoshua), as suggesting a "savior" becomes all the more interesting when

---

[1] "Simon whom he surnamed Peter; James the son of Zebedee and John the brother of James, whom he surnamed Boanerges, that is, sons of thunder" (Mark 3:16-17).

coupled with the term "Christ." Like the word "Jesus," the word "Christ" is more a role or a function than a name.

What do we make then of the name-word "Christ"? This term has more misleading connotations and implications than can be counted. Although I have no statistical proof at hand, I would venture to say that for many the name-word "Christ" is the very word that means "savior," which, of course, is does not. Then too there are those who automatically append the word Christ immediately after the name "Jesus. "One would think that they see it as his last name. While the name-word "Jesus" may have lost any sense of its original meaning, the name-word "Christ" has strayed even farther.

Like the name "Jesus," the term "Christ" has a distinct original meaning that common usage and understanding have all but obliterated. The term "Christ" is the Greek translation of the Hebrew "messiah" or, perhaps more correctly, "meshiyach" (מ ש.יח). In Hebrew, "meshiyach," "meshiah" derives from the word "mashah" which means "anoint." The Greek term "Kristos" (Χριστός) stays true to the meaning of the Hebrew. Kristos or Christos also means anointed. Jerome's Latin translation, however, does not use the Latin version of anointed, "unguentatus," but retains the Greek "Christos," and simply changes the Greek ending "-os" to the Latin ending "-us," rendering the word as "Christus." Here again, as he did with the name "Jesus," Jerome masks the original meaning of the attributive word-name and creates a new name for a distinct individual. In this way Jerome differentiates his "Christ" from any other "anointed." Jerome's Latin translation has completely obfuscated the notion of "anointed:" a masking that continues to this day. No one thinks of the word "Christ" and thinks that it means an anointed king.

Trying to research the scriptures for a more exact meaning of the word-names, Christ and Messiah can be quite problematic. Any occurrence of the words depends on which translation of the scripture one reads and therefore on the mindset of those who created the translation. Just as Jerome seems to pick and choose how he will translate a word, so too does any other translator. Take, for example, the number of times the word name-word "Messiah" is found in the Old Testament. If we look at the King James Version, "Messiah" is found only twice in the Old Testament, Daniel, 9: 25–26 and not at all in the New Testament. Look for "Messiah" in the Revised Standard Version: it is absent from the Old Testament and found twice in the New, John 1:41 and 4:25. When, however, we search for its equivalent "Christ," the results are quite different and, of course, exclusive to the New Testament. The King James Version uses the term "Christ" five hundred and seventy-one times. The Revised Standard Version uses it just a little less, with a count of five hundred and thirty-four times. But, now, do the search using the relatively new translation, the Hebrew Name Version of the English Word Bible. This search returns something quite remarkable. The Hebrew Name Version returns all words of Hebrew origin to their original. The HNV removes the name-word "Christ" completely and with it all its connotations. In its place the HNV reads "Messiah" some five hundred sixty-three times. This return to the original Hebrew casts a very different light on our reading of Jesus and his mission. With the HNV translation, we begin to see a very different and far more meaningful picture.

The seeming arbitrariness of the translation of "Messiah" is not limited to English. Take, for example, the famous verse in Psalm 2, "The kings of the earth set themselves, and the rulers take counsel together, against the Lord and his anointed." Compare the various translations of this passage. As we know, the English reads "anointed." But the verse in the Hebrew text reads "Mashiyach." The Greek Septuagint reads "χριστοῦ" (Christou). Like the English translation of the literal "anointed," Luther's translation also renders the German equivalent of "anointed," "Gesalbten." When it comes to a more scholarly text, we find that in the contemporary French of *La Bible de Jérusalem* it is "Messie."

Why this confusion? Frankly, I have no answer. The study of such complexities belongs to the realm of specialists. But it does seem that in many translations, particularly traditional ones, that there is a concerted attempt to distinguish the word messiah when it is applied to Jesus specifically and when the term is used generically. In any event, the point here is that the term "Christ" is certainly not a name but is a title that speaks of a specific role or function. It refers to a person who is the "messiah" or "anointed": someone who is selected to be a ruling monarch, a king. And in the case of Israel, the anointed king will be the one who will free his people from their enemies.

The term "anointed" literally means to be rubbed or smeared with oil.[1] The practice of rubbing or smearing a person with oil dates back to the most ancient times. The oil, taken from either animal or vegetable sources, contained ritualistic powers that were transferred to the person on whom they were rubbed. In the Old Testament we read how Aaron and his sons were to be anointed priests, "And you shall take the anointing oil, and pour it on his head and anoint him" (Exodus 29:7). Elsewhere in the Old Testament, the altar and other elements of worship were to be anointed: "You shall also anoint the altar of burnt offering and all its utensils, and consecrate the altar; and the altar shall be most holy" (Exodus 40:10). But more important to our investigation was the anointing of the king. Saul the prophet has been sent

---

[1] c.1300 (implied in *anointing*), from Old French *enoint* "smeared on," past participle of *enoindre* "smear on," from Latin *inunguere* "to anoint," from *in-* "on" + *unguere* "to smear"

to the house of Jesse to find the one who is to be the first king of Israel. Jesse brings all his sons before Saul, all except the somewhat forgotten youngest.

> And Samuel said to Jesse, "Are all your sons here?" And he said, "There remains yet the youngest, but behold, he is keeping the sheep." And Samuel said to Jesse, "Send and fetch him; for we will not sit down till he comes here." And he sent, and brought him in. Now he was ruddy, and had beautiful eyes, and was handsome. And the Lord said, "Arise, anoint him; for this is he." Then Samuel took the horn of oil, and anointed him in the midst of his brothers; and the Spirit of the Lord came mightily upon David from that day forward. And Samuel rose up, and went to Ramah. (1 Samuel 16:11–13)

At a much later date, after the fall of the kingdom of Israel, a notion arises that God will send a new king, a new "anointed" one, who will liberate the Jews from their conquerors. It is in this sense of a promised king that we may very well find the meaning of "Messiah" as it was used to describe Jesus. The notion of a promised "messiah" dates from the second century before the Christian era. The term is first found not once but twice in the book of Daniel, an apocalyptic text that looks to a coming new of a new Israel.

The date of the composition of the book of Daniel seems to be something of a debate. But in terms of the overall tone of Daniel, it does not seem to be far removed from the writings of the Qumran community that flourished around two hundred years before and during the time of Jesus. In the Qumran writings we again find the notion of a messiah who will be a king: "The heavens and the earth will listen to his Messiah, and none therein will stray from the commandments of the holy ones ("Messianic Apocalypse" (4Q521)).[1] Here too, the reference to a messiah is to a king who will rule with power and glory.

But here is the essential point. In all of these references the longed for king, the "messiah" or "Christ" who would liberate his people was never seen as the sacrificial victim intended as a blood offering for sin as today's Christians interpret the role. Quite to the contrary, the "Christ" or Messiah was would be a great leader whose strength and divine inspiration would restore the monarchy of his ancestors Saul and David and Solomon.

How then did the term "Christ" or Messiah come to be applied to Jesus and how did this term alter in its meaning of an anointed king to the notion of a sacrificial victim? It would seem that in some kind of desperate attempt to give meaning to the execution of Jesus, his followers began to transform the notion of a messiah, a Christ, from that of a ruler to that of a sacrifice.

---

[1] I leave a full study of the Dead Sea Scrolls and the community at Qumran to others. I do not wish to make unfounded claims about this community and their documents. What I think I can say with relative confidence is that they held some notion of an apocalyptic king or messiah (maybe even more than one of them).who would lead Israel into a new world.

The transformation is most strongly evidenced in the epistles of Paul but continues even to our own day. Few are those Christians who take the time to think of the meaning of the title "Christ." Indeed, I would go so far as to say that the title "Christ" in the minds of most Christians has been muddled into some kind of personal name. It has lost its original meaning completely. Just as Christians have infused the synoptics gospels with the proclamations of love found in John's gospel so too they confuse the meaning of the title "Christ" and invest it with other connotations, connotations that evolve into denotations that the word does not merit. Indeed, as with so many other Christian mis-notions, the problem may very well begin with the epistles of Paul. In Paul's writings he rarely uses the name "Jesus" by itself. Almost every instance of the name Jesus in his epistles is attached either before or after with the appellation "Christ." The two words become almost inseparable. While Paul's Greek-speaking audience may have understood the word "Christ" in its denotative meaning, such is no longer the case. "Christ" has become little more than a synonym for "Jesus."

As to Jesus himself, the first time that he suggests his role as the promised king is in the opening verses of Mark. While Jesus does not say specifically that he is the promised Anointed One, he unabashedly declares that the kingdom is coming, "The time is fulfilled, and the kingdom of God is at hand; repent, and believe in the gospel" (Mark 1:15).[1] Is Jesus here claiming that it is he who is the bringer of this kingdom? In the synoptics just after Jesus has fed the multitude and has cured a blind man he asks his followers, "who do men say that I am?" Peter responds with the words, "You are the Christ (of God)" (Matthew 16: 15–17, Mark 8:27–28, Luke 9: 18–21).

The name-word "Christ" once again hides the words meaning. Reread the Greek "Christ" as "anointed" or "king" and the passage takes on a very different tone. When we read it as "Christ" we understand a concept loaded with other connotations developed well after Jesus' death and elaborated over the past two thousand years. If, however, we read Peter's response not as the "You are the Christ" but as "You are the Anointed," we hear and understand something quite different. To call Jesus the "Anointed One," the "Messiah" is to call him a king. To call Jesus the king, the king of Israel, is nothing short of a treasonous statement, at least in terms of Roman rule. Is this the first indication that this Galilean wonder-worker began having bigger ideas about his mission and about who he was?

In Luke, Jesus makes the claim that he is the Messiah, the promised king, by referencing himself as the meaning of a scriptural passage he has just read in the synagogue.

---

[1] See also Matthew 4:17, Luke 17:21

> And he came to Nazareth, where he had been brought up; and he went to the synagogue, as his custom was, on the Sabbath day. And he stood up to read; and there was given to him the book of the prophet Isaiah. He opened the book and found the place where it was written, "The Spirit of the Lord is upon me, because he has anointed me to preach good news to the poor. He has sent me to proclaim release to the captives and recovering of sight to the blind, to set at liberty those who are oppressed, to proclaim the acceptable year of the Lord." And he closed the book, and gave it back to the attendant, and sat down; and the eyes of all in the synagogue were fixed on him. And he began to say to them, "Today this scripture has been fulfilled in your hearing." (Luke 4:16–21)

The "me" in the Isaiah passage, Jesus clearly identifies as himself. Luke's Jesus is the "Anointed One," sent to "set at liberty those who have been oppressed." Curiously, Mark's Jesus who is otherwise most convinced that he is about to bring about a new kingdom does not find himself in the synagogue setting and consequently does not make this statement. Nor, for that matter, does the Jesus of Matthew.

Retuning to Mark's account of Jesus we find that Jesus' disciples do not necessarily follow him for altruistic reasons but for what they hope to obtain from him: a place of power. Mark tells us that James and John are interested in what their positions will be in the kingdom they believe Jesus will create.

> And James and John, the sons of Zebedee, came forward to him, and said to him, "Teacher, we want you to do for us whatever we ask of you." And he said to them, "What do you want me to do for you?" And they said to him, "Grant us to sit, one at your right hand and one at your left, in your glory." (Mark 10:35–37)

Now, we must acknowledge that the response of Jesus tells them that to have such a place in his kingdom they must be willing to suffer. But the response of Jesus is incidental to what James and John think. The essential point here is that they think Jesus will be the new king of Israel. Did they have good reason to think this way?

Matthew's gospel presents a slightly different version of the same request. In Matthew's account the request does not come from the two apostles, but from their mother. In Matthew, the mother of the sons of Zebedee approaches Jesus to ask him, "Command that these two sons of mine may sit, one at your right hand and one at your left, in your kingdom" (Matthew 20:21). In some respects this version is even more interesting since it does not describe the ambition of the apostles themselves but of the apostles' families. Here we see not the idea of Jesus' inner circle that he was a king, but the view of even the outer circle of his followers.

Of course, it may be very well argued that when Jesus is speaking of a kingdom he is not talking about an earthly kingdom but the kingdom of heaven as Jesus replies to Pilate, "My kingship is not of this world" (John 18:36). Yet, even if that may be Jesus' intention, at least as far as John would propose, that is not what his followers seem to think. In fact even to the very end of his time on earth at the moment of his ascension the disciples of Jesus are still waiting for a real kingdom. "So when they had come together, they asked him, "Lord, will you at this time restore the kingdom to Israel?" (Acts 1:6). At almost every instance the followers of Jesus, if not Jesus himself believe he was the "savior" the "Yehoshua" whom God would send to transform the earth into some kind of heavenly realm where all would be set aright, where there would be peace and justice for all; and most important, where Jesus would rule as the "Messiah," the "Anointed King?" With his twelve apostles at his side Jesus would establish a new kingdom of Israel in the line of David. And in that kingdom he would have his appointed hierarchy of administrators. Why, after all, would he have chosen twelve apostles? Were these twelve not the new twelve judges to correspond to the ancient twelve tribes of the kingdom of Israel?

Luke's Jesus promises his apostles that as recompense for their loyalty they will rule in his new kingdom, "You are those who have continued with me in my trials; and I assign to you, as my Father assigned to me, a kingdom, that you may eat and drink at my table in my kingdom, and sit on thrones judging the twelve tribes of Israel (Luke 22: 28–30). Luke's Jesus then goes on to say, "But now, let him who has a purse take it, and likewise a bag. And let him who has no sword sell his mantle and buy one" (Luke 22.36). Matthew has a passage that resembles Luke's sword buying. "Do not think that I have come to bring peace on earth; I have not come to bring peace, but a sword" (Matthew 10:34). Cleary, this Jesus is not simply the Jesus of love and compassion. This is a Jesus who sees himself and his followers as the ruling force of a new kingdom. Of course, biblical interpretation has often seen this "sword" as a metaphor. But is there anything in the text that suggests it should be read as such? Furthermore, all the gospels tell us that the disciples were indeed armed. It would seem that they did not hear this statement as a metaphor (Matthew 26:51, Mark 14:47, Luke 22:49, John 18:10).

There is also a moment in Matthew when Jesus' followers are somewhat disconcerted about what they will gain in return for their loyalty. At one point, Peter is somewhat anxious about his position. He and the others have given up all they have to follow Jesus. What will they receive in return? "Then Peter said in reply, "Lo, we have left everything and followed you. What then shall we have?" (Matthew 19:27). In the simplest terms, Peter wants to know what his cut will be when the awaited kingdom arrives. He wants to know "what's in it for me?" Matthew's Jesus assures them saying, "Truly, I say to you, in the new world, when the Son of man shall sit on his glorious throne, you who have followed me will also sit on twelve thrones, judging the twelve tribes of Israel" (Matthew 19:28). Here again, this is not the Jesus of love and caring. This is a Jesus who sees himself and his followers as the rulers of a new earthly kingdom.

This Jesus who sees himself as a king is not talking about a sovereignty in the heavenly ethers. Matthew's Jesus [1] is talking about a "new world," a new world on earth that is expected within their own lifetimes. The Jesus of all three synoptics assures his followers, "Truly, I say to you, this generation will not pass away until all these things take place" (Matthew 24: 34, Mark 13:30, Luke 21:32).

Not unlike that passage in Matthew, the Jesus of Luke also promises a reward to his followers. Luke's disciples of Jesus have been arguing amongst themselves. They argue about which of them is the greatest. Luke's Jesus assures them, "You are those who have continued with me in my trials; and I assign to you, as my Father assigned to me, a kingdom that you may eat and drink at my table in my kingdom, and sit on thrones judging the twelve tribes of Israel" (Luke 22:28–30). Luke's Jesus clearly believes that god has endowed him with a kingdom. He is promising his followers specific roles in its governance. Indeed, when we look again at the passages in Mark and Matthew where the question is who will sit at the right hand and who will sit at the left hand of Jesus, the gospel narrators tell us that even this question caused resentment among the others. "And when the ten heard it, they were indignant at the two brothers" (Matthew 20:24). Clearly these men have an understanding that they are following a man who will restore their country. He will restore the throne of David in a new kingdom of Israel where his disciples will rule over the twelve tribes. This Jesus sees himself as the "anointed," the elected of god who is to be a literal king of a new Israel.

The examples given so far that suggest that Jesus thought he was a true king are limited to the synoptics, Matthew, Mark and Luke. But, there are three other examples where Jesus claims kingship that are not limited to the synoptics. These three examples are found in the gospel of John. Now, this is most unusual because the Jesus of John is not at all the same Jesus that we find in the synoptics. He does not speak in simple parables but in complex metaphysical metaphors. He does not drive out demons or concern himself with banal situations: unless of course they are stagings for a higher meaning and purpose such as the wedding at Cana or the raising of Lazarus.

---

[1] To be intellectually honest, it must be noted that the same passage in Mark and Luke promises a reward of eternal life but not of ruling on twelve thrones.

More important, John's Jesus, unlike the synoptics, makes a claim found nowhere else in the New Testament. John's Jesus goes so far as to make claims of divinity. Take for example the passage, "Jesus said to them, 'Truly, truly, I say to you, before Abraham was, I am.'" (John 8:58). The verb form "I am" immediately recalls the words of God to Moses "I am who I am...I am has sent you." Exodus 3:14 The reference is more than clear. This is a Jesus who announces himself to be divine. Indeed John tells us that the Jews, when they heard these words, recognized their implication and immediately picked up stones to attack Jesus for such a blasphemy. (John 8:59).

Elsewhere John's gospel is peppered with similar verses, most of which begin with the words, "I am..." No such claims of divinity or divine powers such as being "the resurrection and the life" (John 11:25) are made in the synoptics. (More remarkable, even Paul, the great proponent of the "Christ," does not mention Jesus as claiming innate divinity by birth.)[1]

As we know, John's view of Jesus is distinctly different from other New Testament texts. So, when we see passages in John that correspond with passages in the synoptic, these passages attract our attention and hint at some element of authenticity. In John's gospel there seem to be three events or situations that he has in common with the synoptics. All three events are most particularly telling when we consider they lend themselves to possibility that Jesus saw himself as the promised king of Israel. The first time that all four gospels agree is on the entrance of Jesus into Jerusalem. The second is when all four evangelists note that Jesus' followers carried weapons. The last and perhaps most significant concordance is around the statement that the criminal charge affixed to the cross on which Jesus was executed identified his crime as follows: "Jesus of Nazareth, king of the Jews." But let us return to the first event that led to the moment of execution.

One of the first events that all four gospels share is the entrance of Jesus into Jerusalem. Jesus' triumphal entrance into the city of David is annually commemorated on Palm Sunday, the Sunday that begins what Christians call Holy Week. Before we consider the momentous quality of this event, it would be helpful to take stock of the situation and its players. We have to look back at the Jesus that the gospels have presented up until his entry into Jerusalem, particularly the image of Jesus as seen in the synoptics. Who was this man making this daring entry into the capital city of Israel, the seat of Roman civil and Jewish religious law? The gospels tell us that Jesus, the wandering preacher, healer, wonderworker and sage, was a Galilean

---

[1] Paul, who mentions nothing of the divine conception of Jesus, seems to say that Jesus becomes the son of God at his resurrection. Paul claims to preach, "the gospel concerning his Son, who was descended from David according to the flesh and designated Son of God in power according to the Spirit of holiness by his resurrection from the dead, Jesus Christ our Lord" (Romans 1:3-4).

from a small town called Nazareth.[1] He was a working man, a carpenter's son[2] (Matthew 13:55), from the northern part of Israel, a fair distance from Jerusalem, that was in the former kingdom of Judah. Jesus, like his disciples, probably spoke with a distinctive northern accent[3] that may have marked him as someone unsophisticated, although as we saw earlier, Luke suggests that he was literate (Luke 4:16).

This Jesus, something of a country person from the North, must have had some kind of moment of enlightenment or revelation. This moment must have encouraged him to greater things. At some point in his career, Jesus was convinced that he was the "Anointed." With that notion fixed in his estimation of himself, this local small-town wonderworker decided that he would lead his followers into the city of David, the capital city of the Jewish people.

But Jesus was not going to Jerusalem simply to visit the temple for the feast of the Passover. His arrival in the Holy City would proclaim to all what only he and his immediate disciples had been discussing about his proposed kingdom to come. There, Jesus would take his place as the promised messiah, the anointed one of god who would restore the ancient kingdom of Israel.

Up until now, Jesus had told his followers not to reveal his true identity to anyone. Only his disciples shared in his ideas. But, then, a change must have occurred. Something emboldened Jesus to announce his calling as the "Anointed One" to his followers, and not just his local followers. Jesus would speak to the nation of Israel at its very center. The Jesus of the synoptics and the Jesus of John decide that it is time to enter the city of Jerusalem. How long it took from the time Jesus began his mission to the actual entering into Jerusalem is not clear. In Christian tradition, Jesus preached his message for about three years. But that tradition is based only in the way one reads the events of the gospel of John. There is nothing in the synoptics that suggests a specific time range for Jesus' career as a prophet. If anything, in the synoptics, it seems that his career was only about one year. The notion of three years comes from John's mention of Jesus attending three Passovers (John 2:13, 6:4, 13:1). But, as we know, the gospel of John, the last of the accepted gospels, was written somewhere around AD 100, a good generation after the supposed life of Jesus. So, his version is the least probable.

---

[1] The question of whether Jesus was truly from Nazareth or that he was rather a member of the Nazarene (Nazorean) sect is immaterial. Our interest is what the text tells us.

[2] τοῦ τέκτονος υἱός, The Greek "tekton" may also mean a person who made things, not necessarily a carpenter.

[3] When Jesus is arrested and Peter creeps into the courtyard where Jesus is on trial. Some suspect Peter of being an accomplice to Jesus, "Certainly you are also one of them, for your accent betrays you" (Matthew 26:73).

Regardless of the number of Passovers that Jesus attended in Jerusalem, the Passover that counts is the last Passover. Whether Jesus came to the full conceptualization that he was the promised Christ or Messiah after one year or after three years matters little. The essential is that there was some point where he was secure enough in his belief about his mission for him to be ready to declare himself publicly in very explicit terms. If we can continue to trust the gospel accounts, it is likewise clear that there was at least some noticeable amount of people to greet his arrival. Can we assume from the crowds who received him that some word of his doings had gone before him? How else can we account for any kind of public reception in the capital city? Emboldened by at least some degree of public support, Jesus determined and staged exactly the way in which he would enter Jerusalem. Jesus looked back to a passage from Zechariah.

"Rejoice greatly, O daughter of Zion! Shout aloud, O daughter of Jerusalem! Lo, your king comes to you; triumphant and victorious is he, humble and riding on an ass, on a colt the foal of an ass." (Zechariah 9:9)

To comply, it would be necessary that he enter the city mounted on a colt (Matthew 21:5, Mark 11:7, Luke 19:35, John 12:15). The synoptics recount that when Jesus decided to enter Jerusalem, he told his disciples to go ahead of him to the village of Bethpage. There, he assured them, they would find a colt of a donkey that they were to bring to him. Should someone question them, they are to say that the colt is for the use of the master. The disciples find the colt and bring it to Jesus. In this way, Jesus fulfills the words of Zechariah, which are apparently viewed as a prophecy, "Rejoice greatly, O daughter of Zion! Shout, O daughter of Jerusalem! Lo, your king comes to you; triumphant and victorious is he, humble and riding on an ass, on a colt the foal of an ass (Zechariah 9:9).[1] (Of course, the original passage in Zechariah, as with all "prophetic" passages, is embedded in a long tirade of violent rhetoric that sounds impressive, but that has little meaning outside its own context.)

Jesus' disciples find the animal and bring it to him. They cover the animal with their cloaks. They have prepared the mount for regal purposes. Jesus makes his entry into Jerusalem, the city of David. Along the roadside, the gospels tell us that at least a certain number of the population have grouped to greet him. Even if the group was rather minimal, they must have been sufficient in number to alert the authorities. They strewd palm branches in his path and acclaimed him with the words "Hosanna to the son of David." With the words "son of David," the people acknowledge Jesus as the

---

[1] It is somewhat comical to note that the author of Matthew read the passage in Zechariah without understanding the poetic repetition of "donkey" and "colt." So, in Matthew they bring not one animal but two, a donkey and a colt.

hereditary heir to the ancient kingdom of Israel. Jesus is the king, the king of the Jews: not Caesar, not Rome, but Jesus. Jesus, a wandering preacher from Galilee, whose followers see him as the Christ, assumes his role as the anointed one, as the king. He is Jesus, Yehoshua, "Savior."

Jesus is making a public display of his self-proclaimed role as the Savior King of Israel. As noted earlier, the entry into Jerusalem also marks that part in the Jesus story where the synoptics and the gospel of John converge in some agreement. With this convergence in mind, and assuming an element of historicity, we cannot ignore the significance of the event in its suggestion of an intended royal if not military arrival.

Look at this situation from the point of view of the Roman authorities and the Jewish hierarchy of the temple. What might their thoughts be? How could they not see this Jesus as anything but a political and religious problem intent on stirring trouble among the populace? The response of the traditional Christian might very well be that this assumption on the part of the Roman authorities and the Jewish priesthood was precisely their mistake in judgment. But when we look at the events of those times, what other conclusions could they possibly draw? This Jesus was not just another prophet from the desert. This was a man who had at least some following in the capital city. Moreover, his arrival was at a time when the authorities surely had enough to do, just to handle the crowds arriving for Passover.

The Jewish historian Josephus, writing a generation after Jesus, provides an idea of the chaos that took place during the feast in Jerusalem.

> While Judaean affairs were under the administration of Cumanus there occurred an uprising in the city of Jerusalem in which many of the Jews perished. I shall first explain the cause from which it was generated. When the feast called the Passover was at hand, at which time our custom is to serve unleavened bread, a great multitude gathered together for it from all parts. Cumanus was afraid lest an attempt at revolution be prompted by their presence, so he ordered one company of soldiers to take their weapons and stand guard in the porticoes of the Temple to repress any attempts of rebellion that might begin. Indeed, this was what previous procurators of Judaea had done at such festivals. (Antiquities of the Jews 20.5.3 106) [1]

While Josephus is referencing an event that took place some thirty years after Jesus, the point to consider is that he suggests that rebellious attacks were generally anticipated. Would not Pilate have been one of the very procurators to whom Josephus is referring?

---

[1] There are also other details recounted, somewhat less appropriate to this study, but they have nothing to do with the point being made. Joseph also notes the recounts the excessive number of people in the city at that time but his figures are certainly exaggerated. See *Wars of the Jews* 2.12.1 224.

But, let's go on to another event in the final days of Jesus, the evening of his arrest. Once again, all four gospels, even John, recount that final evening with the same telling detail: the followers of Jesus were armed!

Later in the week, Jesus is at table with his disciples. Exactly which night that was depends on whether you follow the version in the synoptics or the version related by John.[1] Either way, it is the last night before his execution. After their dinner, Jesus retreats to the Garden of Gethsemane. All four gospels tell us that a detachment of soldiers, directed by the treachery of Judas, has been sent to arrest Jesus. But, curiously, Jesus' disciples are ready in that garden to defend their master with weapons. Why, one must ask, would these men who are supposedly simple followers of a man (whom most Christians think of as the teacher of peace), be armed with weapons?

When the soldiers approach Jesus, Luke tells us that his followers cry out, "Lord, shall we strike with the sword?" (Luke 22:49). So, it would seem from Luke's account that it was not just one of them that was armed but at least a few of them. Not only do they ask if they should defend Jesus with arms, but one of Jesus' followers cuts off the ear of a member of the arrest party (Matthew 26:52, Mark 14:47, Luke 22:51). Oddest of all is the passage in John, the last written of the gospels, where the person wielding the sword is identified as Peter himself, the man who is supposed to be the closest to Jesus (John 18: 10–11).

Now, here is the question. What were these simple men, fishermen and peasants, doing with swords? What in their occupation would require one? Even from a very practical point of view, a sword was a rather expensive item. Weaponry was not something that the average person could afford. So, we must ask from more than one perspective, why would these disciples be armed? In Luke's account of this event, there is an additional remark from Jesus that is nothing short of perplexingly ironic. Luke's Jesus asks the arresting deputation, "Have you come out as against a robber, with swords and clubs?"(Matthew 26:55, Mark 14:48). This is a very odd thing to say, for a man whose followers have just attacked and mutilated one of the guards. Why have they come out with "swords and clubs"? It would seem rather obvious—the first thing that happened to this deputation was that Jesus' followers attacked them and one of them has his ear cut off! Clearly, there was a reason that they came "with swords and clubs." The soldiers were coming to arrest the leader of an armed group. What was it that the soldiers (and those that sent them) knew about Jesus and his followers that may not be immediately evident to us? Could it not be that the deputation was

---

[1] I would opt for the synoptics. John is far too contrived in its attempt at metaphor. See Chapter 5.

going out to stop an armed gang of potential insurgents, a group of men who thought that they were following a rebel king?

The most telling element in the gospels that suggests Jesus believed himself to be the promised king of Israel is the testimony of Jesus before Pilate and Pilate's subsequent verdict as illustrated by the sign to be fixed to the cross: an event that is also found in the synoptics and in John. When reading the four accounts of the trial and crucifixion, the reader senses a very different tone from that of the rest of the gospel stories. There is something in the text that rings of the factual and the historical. We are no longer dealing with a Jesus of different complexions and personalities. Other than the philosophical elaborations in John, all four gospels seem to agree on most of the events. They all paint a Jesus who is a would-be king. The wonder worker, the prophet, the sage are all stripped bare to reveal a man who is accused and executed for crimes against the state.

The death of Jesus begins with his arrest, the details of which we have discussed. Before we present any evidence for this scene, the fundamental question is, if this trial took place in the residence of Pilate and the disciples had all fled, who heard the exchange between Pilate and Jesus? Clearly, the interrogation in all four gospels is entirely invented. The gospel authors have entirely created the scene and the conversation between Pilate and Jesus. Nonetheless, in its invention we may be able to detect something of what Jesus actually thought or at least something of what his followers imagined that Jesus thought. In all four versions of the story, we read that Pilate asks Jesus if he is indeed "king of the Jews." In all four, Jesus admits that he is. This question and this answer are among the very few verses that are the same in all four gospels. For the sake of example, here is Luke's version. "And Pilate asked him, 'Are you the King of the Jews?' And he answered him, 'You have said so.'" (Matthew 27:11, Mark 15:2, Luke 23:3). Pilate's question is direct and unambiguous. All three gospels have Jesus give the same answer, that he is a king. It would seem that Jesus has been arrested because he is seen as a political problem. He has staged a public event that aroused the people where he allowed himself to be called the "son of David," a claim of kingship. As we have seen, his followers carry weapons. In the eyes of the authorities, Jesus is nothing less than a rabble rouser if not an outright revolutionary. To arrest him and execute him is not without political reason.

But we must also look at the scene in John. In John the answer is, in John's typical fashion, far more philosophical. The exchange between the two also contains some interesting other details.

> Pilate entered the praetorium again and called Jesus, and said to him, "Are you the King of the Jews?" Jesus answered, "Do you say this of your own accord, or did others say it to you about me?" Pilate answered, "Am I a Jew? Your own nation and the chief priests have

handed you over to me; what have you done?" Jesus answered, "My kingship is not of this world; if my kingship were of this world, my servants would fight, that I might not be handed over to the Jews; but my kingship is not from the world." Pilate said to him, "So you are a king?" Jesus answered, "You say that I am a king. For this I was born, and for this I have come into the world, to bear witness to the truth. Everyone who is of the truth hears my voice." Pilate said to him, "What is truth?" After he had said this, he went out to the Jews again, and told them, "I find no crime in him." (18:33–38)

This is nothing short of a brilliant scene. Jesus' claim to bear witness to the truth and Pilate's closing words, "What is truth?" sets it among the finest philosophical exchanges. At the heart of the scene however, is the question common to all four gospels, "Are you a king?" So, even as a complete invention of what took place in the trial chamber, there is still that common point of the kingship of Jesus. We have to ask why this would be the case if there was not some grain of truth to it. Of course, in John's version Jesus qualifies his response. In John's scene he adds that his kingdom is not of this world. When we consider the date of John's gospel, this qualification is understandable. In the years immediately following the death of Jesus, they expected a rather immediate return of Jesus. This imminence of his return is quite obvious in the writings of Paul. But by the time of John, a full generation later, the time of the second coming was not so clear. Nor, considering the destruction of Jerusalem by the Romans in the year 70, did it seem that the return would be to restore the kingdom of Israel.

There is also one other somewhat telling detail in John's account. Jesus says "my servants would fight." John seems to have forgotten that in his own account of the arrest, his servants did fight. "Then Simon Peter, having a sword, drew it and struck the high priest's slave and cut off his right ear. The slave's name was Malchus" (18:10).

When we look at all four accounts, even if the events and language of the trial are theatrical inventions, a question remains. Why would the author of the gospels set the question of kingship as the foundation for the trial unless it had at least some element of truth to it? The fact that they all four relate that Jesus was executed for assuming to be the king of the Jews may very well be one of those significant details that reveal more about the truth of the situation than even the gospel writers realized.

The subsequent punishment of Jesus, unlike the trial, may very well be something that had witnesses to inform in some way the gospel composition and the punishment underscores the trial's accusation of Jesus' declaration of claimed kingship. After Pilate has judged Jesus, he turns him over to be flogged. The response of men charged with this torture is most telling. How do they treat their prisoner? The soldiers strip Jesus, cover him in a royal robe and place a crown of thorns on his head (Matthew 61:27–31, Mark 15:16–20, John 19:1–3[1]). As cruel and as violent as this treatment may be, it reflects a sense of vicious satire on the part of the soldiers. In their crude way they mock this village man from the North who thinks he is the king of Israel. Here again there is something in way this scene departs from the often inventive scene in the gospels and moves into details that have a real and historic sense to them. The situation concludes in all four gospels with the written charge against Jesus, to be attached to his cross. Pilate is most clear on the reason for this execution. Each gospel has a slight variation on the phrasing of the charge, but all agree on the fundamental wording, "And over his head they put the charge against him, which read, "This is Jesus the King of the Jews" (Matthew 27:37).

Looking at the events that lead to the crucifixion, considering the name Jesus and the title "Christ" or rather "Messiah" (Anointed One, King), leads to the unavoidable question. Was Jesus executed for politically justifiable reasons? Luke's trial scene gives us the testimony of the Jewish council, "We found this man perverting our nation, and forbidding us to give tribute to Caesar, and saying that he himself is Christ [the Anointed] king" (Luke 23:2). Was there some kind of subversive element in Jesus teachings that the gospels hint at with incidental information but do not relay overtly?

Surely, as we have shown, the death of Jesus makes no sense as a sacrifice to a blood lusting god. There must therefore be a rational reason. Was Jesus little more than an itinerant preacher and supposed wonder worker from a Northern village who eventually took himself for the promised savior of Israel? Was Jesus one of those many voices in the anti-Roman element of the first century that was eventually to collide with the Empire and cause the total destruction of Jerusalem by Titus in the year 70?

With the considerations presented in this chapter, I find myself taking a position on the side of those scholars who believe there was an historical Jesus. If there was, then perhaps he was indeed a revolutionary seeking to establish some kind of new Israel where he and his followers would rule. Perhaps when this Jesus met his fate on the cross as a treasonous rebel, his immediate followers, deluded and confused, gradually developed mystical oral tales to correct and justify the death of their leader. Later still, under the influence of Paul and the successive gospels, the stories reinvented the image and the meaning of their "Messiah," their "Anointed," their "Savior," to become the figure of a newly invented and even mythical history: a mythical history based on a very real person who thought he was the Christ Jesus, the "Anointed Savior" king of Israel.

---

[1] Luke alone does not include this scene.

CHAPTER 10. THE TEACHINGS OF CHRISTIANITY: "GO AND DO LIKEWISE"

In the preface of this book I make a distinction between what I consider Christian doctrines and Christian teachings. I hope that this study has demonstrated that those notions that are held as Christian doctrine are manifestly irrational and untenable. When it comes to what I will call Christian teachings, however, the same is not at all the case.

Among those ideas that I will call Christian teachings are those that have instilled the concepts of community, of kindness, of concern and awareness of ourselves and those around us and the world in which we live. Indeed, I will go so far as to say that many of these concepts came into a fuller sense in our human self-awareness only with the advent of Christian teachings.[1] Most important, I find that all such Christian teachings innately possess intrinsic human values completely independent of any Christian doctrine. I do not need to believe in a blood sacrifice in order to help another human being. I do not need to await the reward of resurrection from the dead to care for the ill or homeless. I do not need to believe in a Messiah king, yet to come, to work towards peace on earth.

In this chapter I would like to examine those Christian teachings that have influenced the world towards the good: teachings that, born in the Church, now stand on their own outside of religious doctrine. In so doing I would like to present certain passages from the New Testament that demonstrate such teachings. In this examination I would also like to look briefly at other points of view that disagree and agree that Christian teachings have a merit of their own.

---

[1] See Stark, Rodney. *How the West Won*: New York, MacCulloch, Diarmaid. *Christianity*, New York, 2009

While it is more than evident that the Christian world has warred and burned and pillaged throughout the past two thousand years, I would contend that in most cases those unforgiveable horrors were more the result of belief in Christian doctrine than belief in Christian teachings. Religious wars in Europe pitted doctrine against doctrine, pope against protestant. Wars of conquest were led by crusaders or conquistadors who sought to plant the cross of Jesus on infidel shores from the Holy Land to the New World. Heretics were burned. Jews were slaughtered or exiled. Dissenters were forced to find refuge in unsettled lands. While it must be admitted that doctrine itself was not always the cause for humankind's propensity for aggressive behavior, it seems that doctrine often provided the armor for the natural tendency for power and greed and intolerance. I would be hard pressed, on the other hand, to find such acts of belligerence motivated by the Sermon on the Mount or the parables of Luke's gospel.

Of course there have been those who might find such Christian teachings as a weakening disease. Among contemporary writers, one of the first that comes to mind is Christopher Hitchens. While there is much in Hitchens with which I agree, when it comes to the rational aspects of atheism, I cannot say that I would subscribe to his thoughts on one's personal rapport with the world. Hitchens seems to subscribe to the writings of the 19th century Friedrich Nietzsche. Hitchens in the closing pages of his *Letters to a Young Contrarian* advises:

> Beware the irrational, however seductive. Shun the "transcendent" and all who invite you to subordinate or annihilate yourself. Distrust compassion; prefer dignity for yourself and others. Don't be afraid to be thought arrogant or selfish. Picture all experts as if they were mammals. Never be a spectator of unfairness or stupidity. Seek out argument and disputation for their own sake; the grave will supply plenty of time for silence. Suspect your own motives, and all excuses. Do not live for others any more than you would expect others to live for you. p. 140 (Hitchens, 2001)

While such advice as shunning the irrational or never being a spectator to stupidity or fearing disputation have sound groundings, there are other parts of this advice that are hard words. Perhaps because I still find myself a cultural Christian, such advice seems not only impractical in terms of interpersonal relationships but rather frightening when we consider its implications on the broad human scale. In many ways, however, Hitchens has put most succinctly into words the foundational notions that we find in the writings of possibly the most famous atheist in Western history.

Friedrich Nietzsche in his claim for the need to return to what he considered the far more noble aspirations of the pre-Christian world vigorously proclaimed,

I should say that Christianity has hitherto been the most portentous of presumptions. Men, not great enough, nor hard enough, to be entitled as artists to take part in fashioning man; men, not sufficiently strong and far-sighted to allow, with sublime self-constraint, the obvious law of the thousandfold failures and perishings to prevail; men, not sufficiently noble to see the radically different grades of rank and intervals of rank that separate man from man:— such men, with their "equality before God," have hitherto swayed the destiny of Europe; until at last a dwarfed, almost ludicrous species has been produced, a gregarious animal, something obliging, sickly, mediocre, the European of the present day. (*Beyond Good and Evil: The Religious Mood*, Chapter 3: 62)

For those such as Nietzsche over a century ago and for those such as Hitchens in our own time the teachings of the man called Jesus produce not a race of "men" but of mindless animals without individual will.

Not all critics of Christianity are as harsh. A century before Nietzsche, one of the fathers of our country, Thomas Jefferson, undertook a personal project not unlike that of this book. Jefferson sought to maintain what I have called the teachings of Christianity while at the same time dismissing the doctrines. Now, it must first be said that Jefferson was a free thinker and possibly a deist. He was a close contemporary of the philosophers Voltaire, Diderot and Rousseau. Like them he was heir to the rationalist minds of Descartes and Pascal. The other enlightened minds of his age would certainly have applauded his words that we read on his monument in the nation's capital, "I have sworn upon the altar of God eternal hostility against every form of tyranny over the mind of man."[1]

Now even though Jefferson used the word "god" in this declaration, whether Jefferson believed in god or not, I will leave to his historians. What we do know is that he sought to liberate the human mind from the irrational notions of dogma and doctrine. What Jefferson thinks of the scriptures containing these doctrines he makes rather clear. In a letter to John Adams he writes,

but the whole history of these books [of Moses] is so defective and doubtful that it seems vain to attempt minute enquiry into it: and such tricks have been plaid with their text, and with the texts of other books relating to them, that we have a right, from that cause, to entertain much doubt what parts of them are genuine. In the New Testament there is internal evidence that parts of it have proceeded from an extraordinary man; and that other parts are of the fabric of

---

[1] The quote is taken from a letter to Benjamin Rush dated September 23, 1800 (The National Archives), decrying certain member of the clergy of Philadelphia for "printing lying pamphlets against me."

very inferior minds. It is as easy to separate those parts, as to pick out diamonds from dunghills. (January 24, 1814)[1]

Jefferson's final imagery is rather strong. Yet, we must pause a moment to see what he may really be seeking in the scriptures. Jefferson wanted to make the same distinction as we do here in this study, to eradicate the irrational notions of doctrine (the dung) and save the "diamonds" of Christian teaching. As one of Jefferson's numerous enterprises and inquiries into countless subjects, one of his most intriguing and personal was his investigation of the New Testament. As a man of reason and of common sense he wanted, as he said, to save the valuable for its great worth and not simply and mindlessly discard it with the useless dross for lack of initiative or interest in undertaking their evaluation.

In an earlier letter to Adams, Jefferson describes in detail the tedious task he has undertaken to liberate the New Testament from all its irrational mysteries, miracles and doctrines. Once cleared of these obstructions, he intends to present a human image of Jesus and his teachings. Speaking of Jesus, Jefferson writes,

> In extracting the pure principles which he taught, we should have to strip off the artificial vestments in which they have been muffled by priests, who have travestied them into various forms, as instruments of riches and power to them. We must dismiss ... nonsense. We must reduce our volume to the simple evangelists, select, even from them, the very words only of Jesus, paring off the Amphibologisms[2] into which they have been led by forgetting often, or not understanding, what had fallen from him, by giving their own misconceptions as his dicta, and expressing unintelligibly for others what they had not understood themselves. There will be found remaining the most sublime and benevolent code of morals which has ever been offered to man.

Jefferson then goes on to point out that he is making physical cuts in his bible and pasting together only those teachings that are rational.

> I have performed this operation for my own use, by cutting verse by verse out of the printed book, and arranging, the matter which is evidently his, and which is as easily distinguishable as diamonds in a dunghill. (Letter to John Adams, October 12, 1813)

Who else but Jefferson would take the time to laboriously page through four bibles, Greek, Latin, French and English, to isolate the verses he found rational, slice them from the books with a razor then tediously glue them one on top of the other to create a new text? It seems that Jefferson completed his project somewhere around 1820 at Monticello.[3]

---

[1] National Archives.

[2] An ambiguous or equivocal statement.

[3] The compilation takes 84 pages of cut and paste text. It runs in four columns, Greek, Latin, French and English. It was acquired in 1895 from his great-granddaughter. The Smithsonian Institute.

He writes to William Short:[1]

> But while this Syllabus is meant to place the character of Jesus in its true and high light, as no imposter himself but a great Reformer of the Hebrew code of religion, it is not to be understood that I am with him in all his doctrines. I am a Materialist, he takes the side of spiritualism; ... I find many passages of fine imagination, correct morality, and of the most lovely benevolence: and others again of so much ignorance, so much absurdity, so much untruth, charlatanism, and imposture, as to pronounce it impossible that such contradictions should have proceeded from the same being. I separate therefore the gold from the dross; restore to him the former & leave the latter to the stupidity of some, and roguery of others of his disciples. Of this band of dupes and impostors, Paul was the great Coryphaeus,[2] and firm corrupter of the doctrines of Jesus. (Letter to William Short, April 13, 1820)

As we read, Jefferson had little regard for Paul. Even as we have noted in this study, it is rather clear that Paul invented the notion of what will be called Original Sin. It is he who contrives the doctrine of the blood sacrifice of Jesus and his resurrection from the dead. It is Paul who, through his epistles, directs his chorus of followers in their irrational dance and song in the redemption mysteries of Jesus from cross to second coming. But, to be fair, it is also Paul who amplifies the notion of Jesus as the teacher of love. It is, however, the rational Jesus, teacher of morals and ethical values, that Jefferson is seeking. In the process Jefferson cuts away the mythical mysteries of the gospels. Jefferson entitles his endeavor, as written in his own hand, *The Life and Morals of Jesus of Nazareth, extracted textually from the Gospels, in Greek, Latin, French & English*. Jefferson never published his bible. He shared it only with close associates.

Jefferson Bible, Title Page, Smithsonian

---

[1] Jefferson's private secretary.
[2] In Greek drama the coryphaeus directed the movement of the chorus or the group.

The Jefferson Bible, Smithsonian Institute

Like Jefferson, this study too would like to preserve the teachings of Christianity that have served as signposts for the advancement of society and civilization and cut away the irrational doctrines that have blinded us in our pursuit of truth. Yes, one can easily accuse such a process as a cunning picking and choosing: a process to serve a personal need or to accommodate a pre-determined goal. But, the very process of the rational mind is that it can pick and choose. Its nature is to discern and in that discernment to separate the wheat from the chaff.[1]

As Jefferson cut and pasted his selected passages, so too I would like to consider at least some of those teachings that may continue to serve humankind with no need of doctrine.

Perhaps the most morally and ethically comprehensive arrangement of Christian teachings are found in the gospel of Matthew when his Jesus addresses the multitude with what is called the Sermon on the Mount or The Beatitudes. When we read such passages, we might easily dismiss the sentiment. The overall tone admittedly sounds somewhat maudlin.

---

[1] Matthew 13:24

Blessed are the poor in spirit, for theirs is the kingdom of heaven.

Blessed are those who mourn, for they shall be comforted.

Blessed are the meek, for they shall inherit the earth

Blessed are those who hunger and thirst for righteousness, for they shall be satisfied.

Blessed are the merciful, for they shall obtain mercy

Blessed are the pure in heart, for they shall see God.

Blessed are the peacemakers, for they shall be called sons of God.

Blessed are you when men revile you and persecute you and utter all kinds of evil against you falsely on my account.

Rejoice and be glad, for your reward is great in heaven, for so men persecuted the prophets who were before you. (Matthew 5:3–12)

Nietzsche would immediately point out that the ultimate reward in these promises is something beyond the rational and physical world. The reward is dependent on "The father" in God (who) is thoroughly refuted; equally so "the judge," "the rewarder" (*Beyond Good and Evil*. Chapter 3:53). Perhaps I would agree with Nietzsche on this point. Perhaps the very problem is that the social teachings in the Sermon are couched in the doctrine of life after death and an eternal reward.

However, if we replace the doctrinal overtones of the text with rational and human values, with no other objective than the wellbeing of the world in which we live, we may find values that address no small number of the problems that humankind has faced—not only in the past but even today. For example, for "blessed," read "thoughtful," or perhaps "wise," and for the rewarder, "god," read "humankind."

While the phrases may be somewhat awkward, their essence is not without merit: "Thoughtful are the merciful, for they shall obtain mercy"; "Thoughtful are the peacemakers for they will be called the children of humankind." These transformations admittedly sound like something from a 1970s peace demonstration or from a "modern language" translation of that era.[1] I myself cringe a bit at having written them. Nonetheless, the social concepts found in such passages moved an entire culture and civilization into a new level of consciousness that was not present in the classical world of Greece and Rome.

It is also in Matthew's Jesus that we find those teachings that will later become the Corporal Works of Mercy.

I was thirsty and you gave me drink,

I was a stranger and you welcomed me,

I was naked and you clothed me,

I was sick and you visited me,

---

[1] Burke, Carl F. *God Is for Real Man.* Hill and Wang, 1966, *The Good News Bible* (*Good News for Modern Man*, NT) Zondervan, 1966.

I was in prison and you came to me.
(Matthew 25: 35–36)

Can it be argued that these teachings do not stand as the groundwork of institutions and practices that have nurtured and grown civilization? Hospitals, schools, asylums and many other social organizations are born from them. How can it be denied that, while not always practiced as they should be, they still stand as reminders of the goals for which we are all responsible? While Christianity are not alone in recognizing the ethical values of these verses, it is in Christian writings that we find them clearly enumerated.[1] I am certainly not well read in the religions of the East, and I have no documentation that other belief systems may or may not share the notions of either the Sermon on the Mount or the Corporal Works of Mercy in their writings. But it would seem to me that the Western world developed the notion of concern for the "other" to a greater extent than did other civilizations. We need only consider the historic and present social situations of such other places on the globe.

There is probably no biblical passage that better dramatizes the Christian teaching of concern for the "other" than Luke's famous parable of the Good Samaritan. In the parable, a lawyer has just asked Jesus what he must do to attain eternal life. Jesus responds with the well-known verse, "You shall love the Lord your God with all your heart, and with all your soul, and with all your strength, and with all your mind; and your neighbor as yourself"(10:27). This verse is also found in Mark 12:29–33. In Mark, however, when he teaches that we must love our neighbor, he couples it with something of a qualifying and evaluative rationale: "to love one's neighbor as oneself, *is much more than all whole burnt offerings and sacrifices.*" In Mark there is a comparative gain value included in the reasoning that somewhat diminishes the value of love as something worthwhile in and of itself. In this sequence Jesus proclaims that while burnt offerings will earn his questioner something unspecified, love for one's neighbor will earn him something even better. In Mark, earning something seems to be the goal. Luke's Jesus, on the other hand, after answering a similar question with the same quotation from Deuteronomy 6:5 does not respond with a series of specific things to do. As we have mentioned in Chapter 7, Luke's Jesus does not merely make pronouncements such as we read in the Sermon on the Mount. Luke's Jesus also quotes the familiar "love God and love your neighbor." Luke's Jesus, however, adds something unique.

---

[1] There are also the five "Spiritual Works of Mercy." To instruct the ignorant. To counsel the doubtful. To admonish sinners. To bear wrongs patiently. To forgive offences willingly. To comfort the afflicted. To pray for the living and the dead. These five, however, have no direct biblical references.

Instead of proffering precepts, he offers a very human examples of what love for one's neighbor actually means. Luke follows with a parable.

> But he [the lawyer who had just asked the question] desiring to justify himself, said to Jesus, "And who is my neighbor?" "A man was going down from Jerusalem to Jericho, and he fell among robbers, who stripped him and beat him, and departed, leaving him half dead. Now by chance a priest was going down that road; and when he saw him he passed by on the other side. So likewise a Levite, when he came to the place and saw him, passed by on the other side. But a Samaritan, as he journeyed, came to where he was; and when he saw him, he had compassion, and went to him and bound up his wounds, pouring on oil and wine; then he set him on his own beast and brought him to an inn, and took care of him. And the next day he took out two denarii and gave them to the innkeeper, saying, "Take care of him; and whatever more you spend, I will repay you when I come back." Which of these three, do you think, proved neighbor to the man who fell among the robbers?" He said, "The one who showed mercy on him." And Jesus said to him, "Go and do likewise." (10:29–37)

Perhaps the most striking part of this parable is the last verse, "Go and do likewise." Luke's Jesus makes no judgment on the Samaritan. There is nothing at the conclusion that speaks about doing good for the sake of a reward in heaven or in the coming kingdom. Jesus simply tells the lawyer, "Go and do likewise." There are no other remunerations. The good deed, the kindness to the "other," is done simply for itself. The *teaching* to "go and do likewise" has no element of Christian *doctrine* in it whatsoever. There is not even a mention of god. This passage may be one of the most human-centered in the bible. It stands as one of the great teachings of Christianity that merits our embrace with all our reason and understanding while we cast aside those doctrines that confuse the mind with irrational clouds.

Yes, the West certainly brought fire and sword wherever it went, but it also brought hospitals and schools, medicine and education. Yes, the West brought slavery and subjugation to many millions of people. But it also taught the equality and dignity of all.

In the end, we must hope that this latter attribute is opening our minds, although slowly, with the possibility that each coming day will be better than the last. I leave it to the reader to reflect on these points. We can embrace the teachings of Christianity. We have outgrown its doctrines.

Chapter 11. Conclusion

At the start of this book I cited the advice of René Descartes on the use of common sense, that it is a faculty not just to be used but to be used well. Now, at the conclusion of this study, I would like to refer to his wisdom again. In his "Discourse" Descartes offers further advice on how to make best use of one's reason and common sense. He proposes four points, the four steps of a method, to assist not just in applying common sense but in applying it well. I summarize and paraphrase those four steps as follows.

He suggests that the first rule in clear thinking is to accept nothing as true except those things that in and of themselves can be evidently seen to be such. The second rule suggests dividing each point to be considered into its simplest forms. Descartes's third point is to then work from the simplest proposition to the most complex and then to find those things which join proposition to proposition. Descartes's final point is to carefully review one's examination for any overlooked considerations.

I hope that I have followed Descartes advice in preparing this text. To comply with the first step, in this study I have placed side by side those things that doctrines invisibly claim as truth against what we visibly know of the universe. To follow the second step is a bit more taxing. While it is often difficult to extract and separate the interlacing questions of many religious topics, every attempt has been made to isolate each into distinct considerations. For the third step I have begun with the foundational story of Genesis and gradually moved through to the more complex notions of Paul and from there to the gospels and finally to the hypothesis of the meaning of the death of Jesus. Then I have made what I hope is a proper review of my work and avoided any unfounded or undocumented propositions.

As Jefferson did when he created his bible by "separating the diamonds from the dross," this book has divided the wheat of Christian teaching from what I consider the chaff of Christian doctrine. I have sought to present an unbiased position in my acknowledgement of the value of Christian teachings to assure that these teachings are not confused with Christian doctrine and cast aside without deserved evaluation.

I would also note that Descartes concludes his four points with words of the greatest hope for the human mind. Descartes believes that if we apply our common sense well and if we follow this simple method of "distinguishing the true from the false,"[1] "there is nothing that the human mind cannot discover." What estimation of human potential can be more uplifting or more promising?

As we conclude this study, let me pose this situation. If the reader at this point still finds my position unfounded, I would suggest this experiment.

For the moment, forget all you know about Christianity. Make an honest attempt to remove it from your mind. Now, imagine that you have just turned on the television. You see a man giving a lecture, a speech. The man tells you that several years ago a new teacher of truth was maliciously gunned down by the police. He tells you that: "He was killed for the new ideas he was going to bring to America. This murdered man would establish a new form of government where all would be brothers, where all would share everything in common. This man would have brought a new world to all of us. Even more, he proclaims, this man was not just someone ordinary. He was sent by God himself to carry out a plan that would save us from our misguided ways.

"Many years ago, at the founding of this country, the founders were proud men. They did not want a god in their government. They rebelled against God's supreme authority. For this pride, God would have nothing to do with this country. But this man would rescue us from the sin of their pride and rebellion of our forefathers. This man would restore the nation to the will of God. And this is why he was gunned down. The authorities feared him. But" (the speaker goes on to say), "the authorities did not know who they were dealing with. This man overcame their malice. He overcame them because he was sent by god. He overcame them by restoring himself to life to prove his divine commission. "Where is he now?" the man asks his audience. "He has been taken away. Because God sent him, God recalled him back to heaven. But, do not fear, because he will come back. He will come down again from heaven to establish once and for all the government that God has sent him to create." Now ask yourself, would you take a moment to believe what this man on the television was saying? Why

[1] "Distinguer le vrai d'avec le faux."

wouldn't you believe it? Do you not find it perfectly rational? Does it not make perfect sense?

If reading the preceding chapters of *Reason and Doctrine* has accomplished its intent, you have taken a moment to step back from Christianity's doctrines to view them with a rational and questioning eye. You have opened your eyes to reason, eyes that have been blindfolded by a faith that you have accepted without true and honest consideration. It cannot be denied that what we have accepted in faith's doctrines simply cannot stand when viewed in the light of what we know of the world in which we live. The story of the Fall, the foundation of the Christian redemption cycle is nothing more than a myth. The notion that there was a time in human history when humankind did not know death is untenable. The concept of a vengeful god who demands a blood sacrifice is not only repulsive to the civilized world, it is an affront to reason. The belief in the resurrection of the dead and an ascension into a heavenly realm above the earth is little more than the most primitive wishful thinking. It contradicts the order of the physical universe. All the doctrines and dogmas that devolve from the notions mentioned above are subsequently equally impossible.

Even apart from the undeniable arguments of reason, the scriptures themselves reveal that doctrine is founded on errors, misreadings and misconceptions. The unbiased reader will see that there is not one Genesis tale of creation but two. Subsequently Paul has ignored the tale of blessing and selected only the myth of death and banishment as the foundation for his theology. When we look at the gospels we see that they are not consistent. The evangelists have no single version of the teachings of Jesus. The Jesus of Mark is a far different creation than the Jesus of John. The Jesus of Luke teaches in a far different way that the Jesus of Matthew. Even more telling is that the Jesus of Paul knows next to nothing of the Jesus of the gospels.

And what of Jesus himself? What can we actually know of him? What was the cause of his death, and did that death have any purpose? That Jesus was indeed crucified by the Romans hardly seems to have anything to do with an imagined blood lust of a vengeful god. It would seem that in all likelihood Jesus was executed for valid political reasons from the Roman point of view.

Yet, despite the blatant fallacies of Christian doctrines, I find that I must still ask myself a highly important final question. Can we preserve the Christian ethic, as I have proposed in the previous chapter, without Christian doctrine? Even with full rational realization of the impossibilities and absurdities of Christian doctrine, there is great merit to what I have called Christian teaching. From a personal and practical perspective, it is not easy to cast aside the Christian teachings of our childhood and the Christian cultural milieu of adulthood that form us. These formative influences are grounded in a Christian tradition over two thousand years old. Indeed, the Western Tradition from the time of Jesus to the present is inseparable from Christianity. The modern world is born from the literary, artistic and social seeds sown, harvested and resown over the generations in the soil of Christianity. The Christian milieu has given us the genius of the Western world's greatest artists, musicians and authors. Christian values have inaugurated our political aspirations and endeavors. Yes, the Church has also been the fires of the Inquisition and the sword of the Crusades and the blind mindlessness of censorship and bigotry. But these offenses are more the result of Christian doctrine coupled with the innate flaws of humankind.

Despite Paul's otherwise impossible inventions about Jesus, I turn to him for what may be the most significant passage that sums up Christian teaching as opposed to Christian doctrine: "If I speak in the tongues of men and of angels, but have not love, I am a noisy gong or a clanging cymbal" (1 Corinthians 13–1). For the image of the "tongues of men and angels," read the "complexities of Christian doctrines": irrational doctrines that have all too often obfuscated the teaching of love. We cannot deny the value of such a perspective on the importance of concern for one another.

Indeed it was probably in no small measure that Paul's message of love was the tipping point that favored the rise of Christianity. Such a notion concerning love for one's fellow was novel to the ancient world of Greece and Rome. It was contrary to all the values of classic heroic literature. It was, however, an ethic that sparked not only a conversion of the masses but a rising of collective social consciousness. The notion of love for one another is indeed characteristic of the finest and most noble endeavors of our civilization.

We can no longer ignore those aspects of Christianity that confront reason and understanding. "Ignorance is bliss," advises the old adage. And it would seem that many Christians today prefer to remain blissful. If we are going to raise our consciousness, we must move to set aside the myths of Christian doctrine and embrace instead its social teachings unencumbered by irrational and impossible fantasies. We must, as Descartes proposes, apply our reason rightly. Are we secure enough and mature enough to recognize that Christian doctrines are the remnants of primitive explanations born from fear and unknowing and turn ourselves to rationally accept the human condition for what it is? Can we build a house on the stone of reason and intellect and let the waters of superstition and the waves of myth be washed away with the house built on sand?

Ardmore, 2016

Partial Bibliography and Notes on References

Biblical Citations

For ease of transfer and accuracy, biblical quotations have been taken from the online source

Blue Letter Bible. The site offers numerous translations including the two most commonly used in this book, The Revised Standard Version and The Hebrew Names Version.

Early Church Fathers and other historical works

References from the early church fathers and other classical texts have been taken from online sites such as, the Christian Classics Ethereal Library, Early Christian Writings, The Guttenberg Project, and the Perseus Project. Citations from Thomas Jefferson's correspondence are from National Archives.gov and from The Library of Congress.

Printed Bible Editions

The King James Version of the Bible, 1612, The Revised Standard Version
The Jerusalem Bible
La Bible de Jérusalem
La Biblia Sacra
Novum Testamentum
The Tanakh

Books

Armstrong, Karen *The Battle for God*. New York: Random House, 2000.

——. *A History of God*. New York: Ballantine Bo oks, 1993.

Barnstone, Willis, ed. *The Other Bible*. Harper San Francisco

Brown, Peter, *Through the Eye of a Needle*. Princeton University Press, 2012.

Carrier, Richard. *On the Historicity of Jesus*. Sheffield Phoenix Press, 2014.

Dawkins, Richard. *The God Delusion*, Houghton Mifflin, 2008.

Ehrman, Bart D. *Did Jesus Exist*. Harper One, 2012.

——. *How Jesus Became God*, Harper One, 2014.

——. *Misquoting Jesus*, Harper Collins, 2005.

——. *Peter, Paul and Mary Magdalen*. Oxford, 2006.

Hitchens, Christopher. *God is not Great*, Hachette, 2007.

——, *Letters to a Contrarian*, New York: Basic Books, 2001

James, William, *The Varieties of Religious Experience*. Seven Treasures, 2007.

Mac Culloch, Diarmaid, *Christianity*. New York: Viking, 2009

Stark, Rodney, *How the West Won*. Intercollegiate Studies Institute, 2014.

Taylor, Charles, *A Secular Age*. 2007

Wright, Robert. *The Evolution of God*, New York: Little, Brown, 2009.

Index

Printed in the United States
By Bookmasters